Bridgebuilding Equipment of the Wehrmacht 1939-1945

A 16-ton bridge over the Maan, built by German engineers during the French campaign of 1940.

Horst Beiersdorf

Schiffer Military/Aviation History
Atglen, PA

Acknowledgments

I would like to thank my sons Holger and Ulrich, as well as the Wehrbereichsbücherei II in Hannover for their support in bringing this book into being.

In addition, I offer hearty thanks to Reinhard Frank (RF), Randolf Kugler (RK), Horst Scheibert (PzP), the Bernard & Graefe publishing house of Bonn (B&G), and the Bundeswehr Pionierschule in Munich (PS), who made photos and information available.

Bibliography

Service Manuals of the Wehrmacht (H. Dv.+D.)

Petter: Pioniere, Entwicklung einer deutschen Waffengattung,

Podzun-Pallas: 5.I.D., 35.I.D., 44.I.D., 72.I.D., 215.A.D., 19.Pz.D.

Die Wehrmacht: Sturmmarsch zur Loire

Zigaretten-Bilderdienst: Die deutsche Wehrmacht

A squadron of cavalrymen on an eight-ton pontoon bridge of B material, on the advance in Russia.

COVER PICTURE: Engineers building a pontoon bridge of B material.

Translated from the German by Ed Force

Printed in China.
ISBN: 0-7643-0571-9

This book was originally published under the title, *Waffen Arsenal-Kriegsbrückengeräte Der Wehrmacht* by Podzun-Pallas Verlag.

We are interested in hearing from authors with book ideas on related topics.

Published by Schiffer Publishing Ltd.
4880 Lower Valley Road
Atglen, PA 19310
Phone: (610) 593-1777
FAX: (610) 593-2002
E-mail: Schifferbk@aol.com
Please write for a free catalog.
This book may be purchased from the publisher.
Please include $3.95 postage.
Try your bookstore first.

Foreword

In this book the military bridge equipment of the engineer bridge columns will be described. The men of these troops belonged to special units of the Wehrmacht that have scarcely been reported on, but on which all the other service arms depended, for without these engineers, fast marching movements would have been impossible. Even in the already published volumes of the Weapon Arsenal, only little has been written about them.

ENGINEERS

The main task of the engineers is to further the movements of their own troops. For this purpose, the German Wehrmacht had troop engineers and independent engineer battalions in the infantry, mountain, Jäger, paratroop, armored and light divisions. In all areas of action there were multitudes of natural and artificial hindrances to be overcome. Among them, waterways, from narrow brooks to broad streams and mighty rivers played a major role. The engineers made crossing them possible in two ways: by utilizing the military bridging materials carried by the engineer bridge columns, and by using makeshift equipment.

ENGINEER BRIDGE COLUMNS

The bridge columns, as a rule, belonged to the engineer battalions of the divisions. The structure of the battalions consisted of three companies and one bridge column, and these were fully or partly motorized, depending on the division to which they belonged. In partly motorized battalions the first and second companies were marching companies with horsedrawn vehicles while the third company and the bridge column were motorized.

A bridge column on the way to the Dniestr in World War I.

Military Bridging Equipment

To cross waterways, the following bridging materials were used:

A MATERIAL =
whole pontoons taken over from World War I and the Reichswehr, carried by Pontoon Wagon Pf. 8 and Pontoon Wagon Pf. 9, horsedrawn, makeshift motorized, or motorized.

B MATERIAL =
half pontoons, carried by Trestle Wagon Pf. 10, Pontoon Wagon Pf. 11 and Ramp Wagon Pf. 12, motorized, horsedrawn use was possible.

C MATERIAL =
light half pontoons, carried by Trestle Wagon Pf. 14 and Pontoon Wagon Pf. 16, motorized, horsedrawn use was possible.

D MATERIAL =
for reconnaissance units (mot), loaded onto trucks.

G MATERIAL =
mountain bridging device.

H MATERIAL =
Herbert Material. Heavy self-carrying bridges with pontoon support. Taken over from the Austrian and Czech Armies.

I MATERIAL =
device for heaviest loads with pontoon support.

K MATERIAL =
light self-carrying bridge of box materials, supported on three-part pontoons or trestle, carried on trucks.

IZ MATERIAL =
light dismantlable bridges, self-carrying, loaded on trucks.

sS MATERIAL =
heavy ships' bridge.

T MATERIAL =
Czech bridge device. Whole pontoons, carried on trestle or pontoon wagons, horsedrawn or motorized.

Bässler Bridge=
bridge material with swinging trestle (Wurfbock) as fixed support, loaded on trucks.

A pontoon bridge of A material, used by the Reichswehr in 1930. On the bridge is a horsedrawn bridge wagon. Outboard motors are attached to the first two pontoons. (B&G-V)

Bridge Material A
(Described as in H.Dv.222/II)

BRIDGES
With the equipment of a bridge column, rowed ferries could be built of:
- 2 pontoons with 5 planks and simple attachments, load limit 3 tons
- 2 pontoons with double attachments, load limit 4 tons
- 3 pontoons with 9 planks and double attachments, load limit 7 tons

PONTOON:
26 pontoons belonged to a bridge column. They were made of zinc-plated sheet steel. In front, over the front [Kaffe], was a raised part called the spring, which was 0.25 m high at the front and, gradually becoming lower toward the back, measured 1.55 m in all. The rounded end of the pontoon was called the rear [Kaffe]. The bottom of the pontoon was protected externally by 6 sliding bars, each side by one wooden protector.

The pontoon was 8 meters long from end to end, 1.50 m wide at the top, and 0.85 m high at most.

Its weight was about 532 kilograms.
In quiet water, the pontoon had the following heights in the middle:

-unburdened	79 cm
-with a 500 kg load	74 cm
-with a 6000 kg load	22 cm

TRESTLE DEVICE:
This included eight spars of pine or pitch-pine wood. They were 4.11 meters long, 0.32 m high and 0.10 m wide. Each weighed about 90 kilograms.
Sixteen trestle legs were required. The trestle leg made of pine was 4.50 meters long and 10-15 cm thick. It had an iron-covered foot at the bottom, onto which the footplate was stuck. It weighed about 35 kilograms.

A bridge column during a marching pause. The horsedrawn pontoon wagon could be motorized in a makeshift way with a Komnik tractor.

A Trestle Wagon (Pf. 8) is towed through rough country by a Maffei Type MSZ 201 tractor. The tractor could ride on either rear wheels or halftracks. (RK)

The trestle spar carrier was the supporting link between the spar and the trestle leg. It weighed about 40 kilograms. Eight pairs were carried. The footplate, made of ash wood, 0.07 meter thick, with 0.45 and 0.30 meter diamater, served to hold the trestle legs. Sixteen footplates were among the equipment.

PLANKS:
The shore planks (eight of them were on hand) were 4.10 meters long and had a hole at each end for a locking pin. Each weighed 40 kilograms.

The crash planks (56 of them) were 4.75 meters long, 0.15 m high and 0.10 m wide. They weighed 45 kilograms. They linked the shore planks with the trestle spars.

The spike planks (140 of them) were 6.10 meters long, 0.15 m high and 0.10 m wide. They weighed 50 kg. They were laid from pontoon to pontoon.

PLANKS:
The planks (630 of them), made of pine, were 3.75 meters long, 0.26 m wide and 0.035 m thick, and were used to cover the planks. The roadway over the pontoon bridge was made of them.

The weights cited here show that hard work was demanded of the engineers, and often enough it was done under enemy fire.

The Trestle Wagon (Pf. 8) was almost identical to the Pontoon Wagon (Pf. 9), so that if necessary, pontoons could also be loaded onto the Trestle Wagon. D 600)

Pontoon No. 7 of Engineer Battalion 4 of Magdeburg is carried to the water. One NCO and twenty men were required to do the job.

Practice on the Oder in 1930 for Engineer Battalion 3 of Küstrin. On a seven-ton ferry, an armored scout car replica of the Adler Standard 6 type is carried across the river. (RF)

A ferry of Engineer Battalion 5 of Ulm is seen on the Danube. At the lower right, one leg of a trestle with its struts can be seen. (PzP)

Bridge Material B
(Described as in H.Dv.220/3b)

BRIDGES:
The bridges generally consisted of a fixed and a floating part; supports in the fixed part are trestles, in the floating part half or whole pontoons, depending on the type of bridge; ramp parts or crossing parts linked the fixed with the floating parts of the bridge. Bridges that are built only on fixed supports are called trestle bridges.

With the equipment of a Bridge Column B, the following can be built:
- 8-ton bridges to a length of 83 meters,
- 16-ton bridges to a length of 54 meters.

Possible bridge widths are:
- trestle and pontoon stretches: 3.20 meters,
- ramp parts, new type: 3.14 meters,
- ramp parts, old type: 2.90 meters.

Eight-ton bridges were built on half-pontoons. Trestle and pontoon stretches had eight stretch carriers, two rack carriers, two underpieces and a simple covering; they had a doubled covering. Trestle stretches had twelve stretch carriers, two rack carriers and two underpieces, pontoon stretches had 14 stretch carriers, four rack carriers and three underpieces.

FERRIES:
According to how they are used, one differentiates:
- Crossing ferries, ferries to meet bridges, ram and inclusion ferries.

According to their means of motion:
- Rowed ferries, motor ferries, trail or cable ferries.

From Bridge Material B, the following could be built:
- 4-ton ferries,
- 8-ton double ferries,
- 8-ton simple ferries,
- 16-ton ferries,

as well as four-ton ferries and eight-ton simple ferries with the accessory equipment.

When no land bridges were being built, the following were needed for loading and unloading ferries:
- 2 crossing rails for vehicles and single-[p.9]tired motor vehicles.
- 4 crossing rails for horses and double-tired motor vehicles.

BRIDGE WAGONS:
The bridgebuilding equipment was carried on the
- Trestle Wagon (Pf. 10),
- Shore Plank Wagon (Pf. 10),
- Pontoon Wagon (Pf. 11),
- Ramp Wagon (Pf. 12).

The bridge wagons were set up to be towed by motor vehicles or (six) horses. They were equipped with air-pressure, expansion or rider brakes. For horsedrawn use, each wagon carried a shaft, front [Bracke] and [Ortscheite].

MOTORBOAT:
The motorboats (M-Boats) were used to tow and push ferries and bridge members, particularly in crossing and bridgebuilding. They could also be used for towing water vessels for longer distances, as well as individual vehicles for scouting, guarding and similar tasks.

The trailer for the M-Boat (Sd. Ah. 13) was a single-axle trailer for motor vehicles, used for transporting the M-Boat over land. It carried apparatus for moving the loaded M-Boat from the riverbank into the water, or bringing it our of the water.

The crew of an M-Boat when in single use consisted of:
- 1 boat leader (simultaneously steersman). He had to hold a helmsman's license; and
- 1 boatman.

EQUIPMENT
The equipment of a Bridge Column B consisted of:
- 16 half-pontoons,
- 8 trestles,
- 2 ramps,
- 8 shore planks,
- 8 16-ton crossing rails,
- 2 motorboats.

MOTOR VEHICLES OF A BRIDGE COLUMN B

Left: the 5-ton Medium Towing Tractor (Sd. Kfz. 6) with engineer body by Büssing-NAG or Daimler-Benz L 5, L 6 or L 7, built 1935-1937. (D 600)

Right: the 5-ton Medium Towing Tractor (Sd. Kfz. 6) with engineer body, Daimler-Benz L 8 or Büssing-NAG L 8 or L 9, built 1938-1943. (D 600)

(733) Br.Kol. B (mot)

Gruppe Führer:

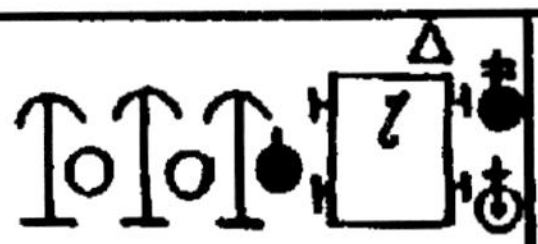

1. u. 2. (Pont.) Zug je:

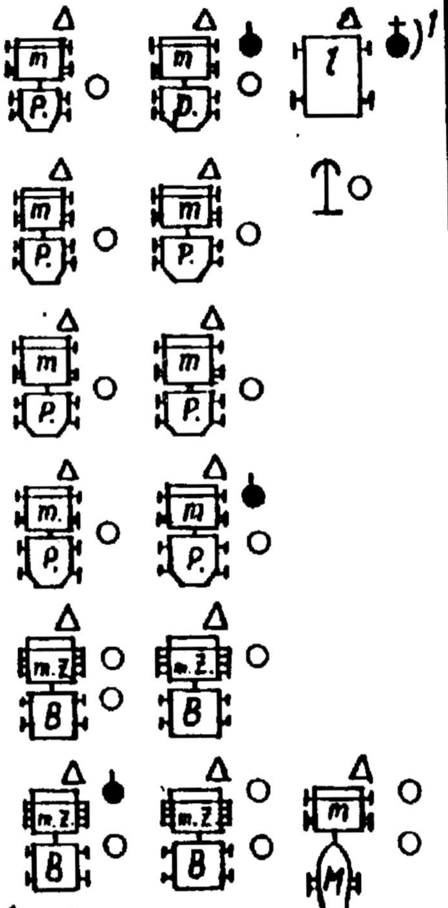

)[1] beim 2.Zug

Ergänzungszug:

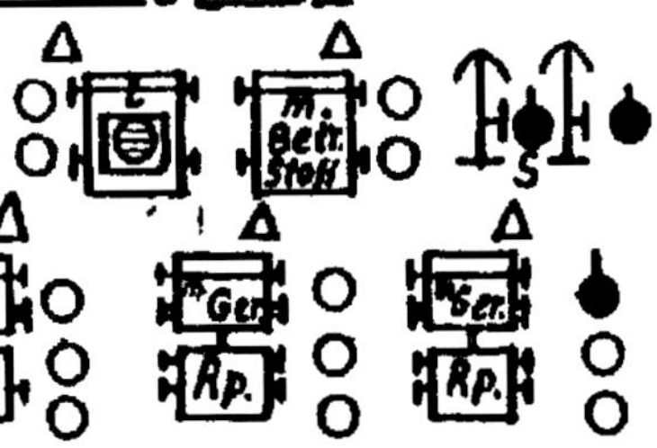

V.- u. G.-Tr.

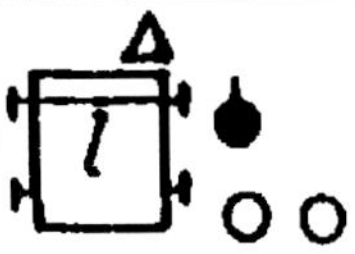

Gesamtstärke:

2 Offiziere, 21 m.gl. Lkw.,
13 Unteroffiziere, 8 " Zg.Kw.,
87 Pioniere (dav. 39 Krflf.), 3 l. Pkw.,
2 l. Lkw.,
29 Anhänger (16 Pont, 8 Bock, 1 m. Lkw.,
2 M-Boote, 1 Fährs., 7 Krad (dav. 2 m.
2 Rampen), 6 Aubos. Beiw.)

Marschlänge im Halten: Ganze Kolonne

ohne V.u.G.-Tr.:	rd.	620 m
Ponton-Zug:		260 m
Erg.Zug:		70 "
V.u.G.-Tr.:		10 "

Nachr.Gerät u. Leistungsfähigk.:

1 Sprechstelle, 1000m l. Feldkabel,
2 Satz Flußkabel (insges. 2000 m)

Gerät der Br.Kol. B (mot)

	~~alt~~	neu:
Übersetzmittel:		
Kl. Floßsäcke	~~20~~	~~56~~ 48
Gr. "	~~24~~	~~8~~ 24
Sperrmittel:		
K.-Rolle	~~12~~	12

Personal nicht z. Bedienen, sondern zur Pflege u. Verwaltung des Geräts. Im Frieden nur Geräte-Einheit, kein Personal.

Medium off-road-capable truck (6x4), Henschel Type 33 D 2 or 33 G 1, built 1937-1942 (D 576/1).

BRIDGE WAGONS AND SPECIAL PONTOON-PLATOON TRAILERS

Left: Engineer Vehicle 10 (Pf. 10) Trestle Wagon. Shore Plank Wagon (D 600).

Engineer Vehicle 11 (Pf. 11), Pontoon Wagon (D 600).

Special Trailer 13 (Sd. Ah. 13) for the 100 HP Motorboat (D 600).

TRAILERS OF THE REPLACEMENT PLATOON

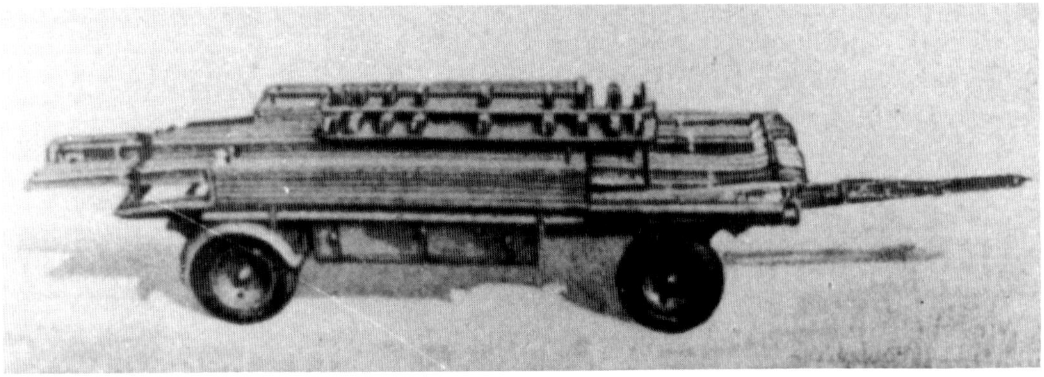

Engineer Vehicle 12 (Pf. 12) Ramp Wagon (D 600).

Special Trailer 15 (Sd. Ah. 15) Trailer (one axle) for ferry cable (H. Dv. 220/ 3a).

Bild 1.
Beladung eines Bockwagens.

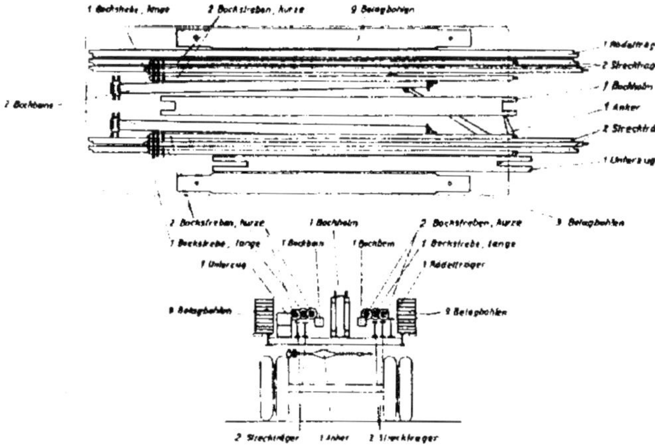

1. Beladeplan für einen Bockwagen (Pf. 10). (Bild 1.)

Stückzahl	Benennung	Bemerkung über die Verladung
	1. Auf dem Wagen	
2	Ankertaue	im Bild 1 nicht eingezeichnet
18	Belagbohlen	in 2 Stapeln verladen
2	Bockbeine	in besonderen Verladevorrichtungen festgelegt
1	Bockholm	
2	Bockstreben, lang	
4	Bockstreben, kurz	
1	Rödelträger	
4	Streckträger	
1	Unterzug	
	2. Am Wagen	
2	Anker	in der Ankerschurre auf der Rückseite[1])
	3. Im linken Gerätekasten	
6	Bindeleinen	
2	Bockwinden mit Kurbel	Kurbel umgesteckt
4	Fenderhaken	
2	Fußscheiben	
2	Fußspitzen	
2	Halteleinen	
1	Sprachrohr	
	4. Im rechten Gerätekasten	
2	Einheitslaternen im Laternenkasten (Pi)	
1	Fettpresse für Bockwinden	im besonderen Einschiebekasten
10	Handbeilen	
	Außerdem Fahrzeugzubehör gem. K. A. N. (H) Nr. 0733 am Fahrzeug und im rechten Gerätkasten.	
	Gesamtgewicht des Bockwagens .... 4840 kg	
	Leergewicht des Bockwagens .... 1920 kg	

[1]) Im Bild 1 nur ein Anker eingezeichnet.

Bild 2.
Beladung eines Uferbalkenwagens.

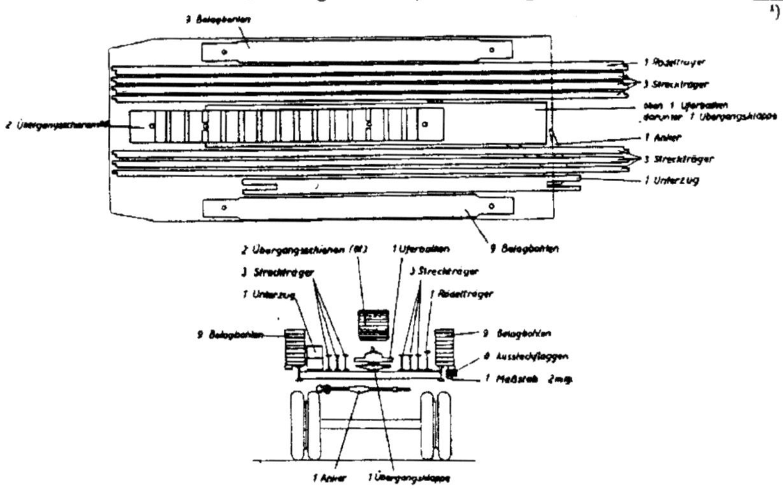

2. Beladeplan für einen Bockwagen (Pf. 10) als Uferbalkenwagen. (Bild 2.)

Stückzahl	Benennung	Bemerkung über die Verladung
	1. Auf dem Wagen	
2	Ankertaue	im Bild 2 nicht eingezeichnet
18	Belagbohlen	in 2 Stapeln
1	Rödelträger	
6	Streckträger	
1	Sperrflagge	auf der Beladung mit 1 Bindeleine festgeschnürt
1	Übergangsklappe	für Fährbetrieb, unter dem Uferbalken verladen
2	Übergangsschienen (8 t)	auf hochklappbarem Gestell
1	Uferbalken	
1	Unterzug	
	2. Am Wagen	
1	Anker	in der Ankerschurre auf der Rückseite
6	Aussteckflaggen mit Laternenhalter	rechte Fahrzeugseite in Beschlägen unter dem Trittbrett
1	Meßstab, 2 m lang	
	3. Im linken Gerätekasten	
4	Geländerpfosten	
2	Halteleinen	
3	Kreuzhacken, lange	
1	Richtleine mit Haspel	
8	Rödelzangen	
4	Schlegel, eiserne	
3	Spaten, lange	
6	Tafeln für Aussteckflaggen	
20	Uferbalkenpfähle	

Stückzahl	Benennung	Bemerkung über die Verladung
	4. Im rechten Gerätekasten	
2	Einheitslaternen im Laternenkasten (Pi)	im besonderen Einschiebekasten
1 Satz	Einfahrzeichen	
1	Wasserwaage	
3	Bindeleinen	
	Außerdem Fahrzeugzubehör gem. K.A.N. (H) Nr. 0733 am Fahrzeug und im rechten Gerätkasten.	
	Gesamtgewicht des Uferbalkenwagens 4840 kg	
	Leergewicht des Uferbalkenwagens . . 1920 kg	

3. Beladeplan für einen Pontonwagen (Pf. 11).
(Bild 3.)

Stückzahl	Benennung	Bemerkung über die Verladung
	1. Auf dem Wagen	
2	Ankertaue[1])	über den Streckträgern mit 2 Bindeleinen festgeschnürt
18	Belagbohlen	in 2 Stapeln verladen
2	Dornplatten	in besonderen Verladevorrichtungen festgelegt
1	Halbponton (Inhalt s. 2)	
1	Rödelträger	
2	Rüstungsträger	
1	Scherhaken	
1	Stoßkappe	
4	Streckträger	
1	Übergangsschiene (8 t)	
1	Unterzug	

[1]) Im Bild 3 nicht eingezeichnet.

Bild 3.
Beladung eines Pontonwagens.

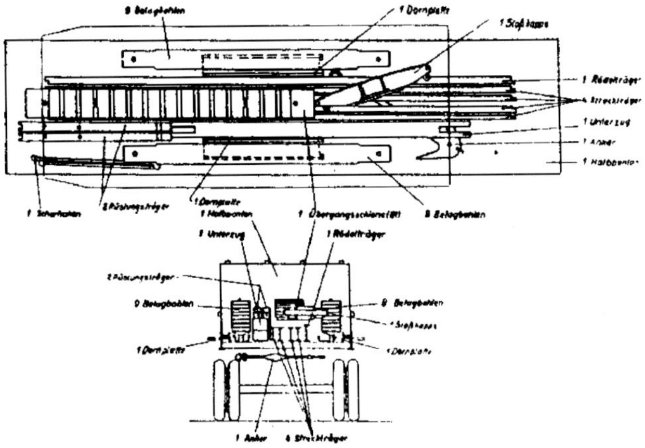

Bild 4.
Verladen des Kleingeräts in die Kaffenkästen.

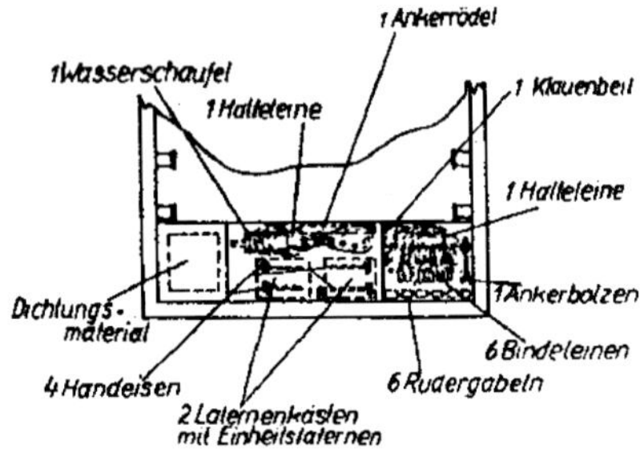

Bild 5. Rampenwagen neuer Art.

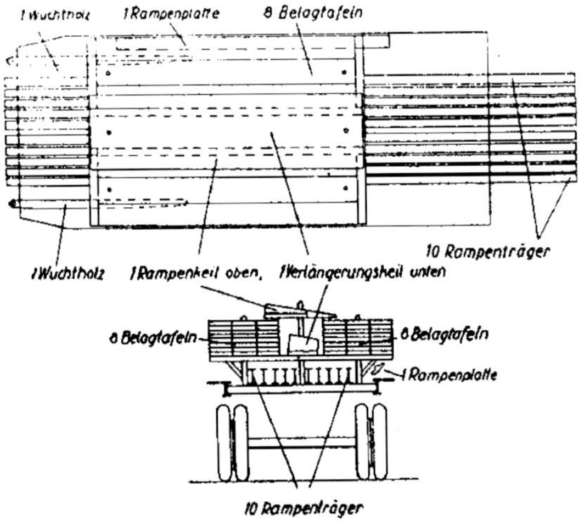

Stückzahl	Benennung	Bemerkung über die Verladung
	2. Im Halbponton	
6	Ruder	mit 2 Bindeleinen an den Vorbwänden festgelegt
3	Staken	
1	Halteleine	am Stevenbügel (Vorderkaffe) angestochen und am Duchtrohr befestigt
1	Beutel mit Dichtungsmaterial	im rechten[1]) Kaffenkasten (Bild 4)
1	Ankerrödel	im mittleren[1]) Kaffenkasten (Bild 4)
2	Einheitslaternen mit Laternenkasten (Pi)	
1	Halteleine	
4	Handeisen	
1	Wasserschaufel	im linken[1]) Kaffenkasten (Bild 4)
1	Ankerbolzen	
6	Bindeleinen	
1	Halteleine	
1	Klauenbeil	
6	Rudergabeln	
	3. Am Wagen[2])	
1	Anker	in der Ankerschurre auf der Rückseite
1	Pontonrolle (Fahrzeugzubehör)	rechte Fahrzeugseite unter dem Trittbrett

[1]) Blick zur Spiegelwand des Pontons.
[2]) Die Motorzug-Gabel wird bei Pferdezug unter dem Fahrzeug, von vorn gesehen links über der Vorderachse umgekehrt eingehängt und verbolzt.

Stückzahl	Benennung	Bemerkung über die Verladung
	4. Im linken Gerätekasten	
2	Deckschrauben	Verteilung auf die einzelnen Fächer s. Plan auf Innenseite des Kastendeckels
2	Geländerpfosten	
1	Rettungsring mit Leine	
2	Rödelzangen	
2	Spannseile	
2	Stoßzangen	
2	Unterzugzangen	
	Außerdem Fahrzeugzubehör gem. K.A.N. (H) Nr. 0733 am Fahrzeug und im rechten Gerätkasten.	
	Gesamtgewicht des Pontonwagens .. 5025 kg	
	Leergewicht des Pontonwagens .... 1900 kg	

4. Beladeplan für einen Rampenwagen (Pf. 12) (Rampenstrecke neuer Art)

(Bild 5).

Stückzahl	Benennung	Bemerkung über die Verladung
	1. Auf dem Wagen	
16	Belagtafeln	in 2 Belagstapeln
1	Rampenkeil	auf Auffahbock
10	Rampenträger	
1	Verlängerungskeil	über dem Rampenkeil verladen
2	Wuchthölzer	Gabel wird über dem vorderen Querträger des Fahrzeuges mit dem Bolzen des Wuchtholzes festgelegt
	2. Am Wagen	
1	Rampenplatte	rechte Fahrzeugseite unter dem Trittbrett
	3. Im linken Gerätekasten	
6	Bindeleinen	
2	Halteleinen	
2	Zugseile zum Ausschieben der Rampenstrecke	
	Außerdem Fahrzeugzubehör gem. K.A.N. (H) Nr. 0733 am Fahrzeug und im rechten Gerätekasten.	
	Gesamtgewicht des Rampenwagens (Rp. Str. n./A.) .... 5600 kg	
	Leergewicht des Rampenwagens ... 1900 kg	

Bild 6.
Rampenwagen alter Art.

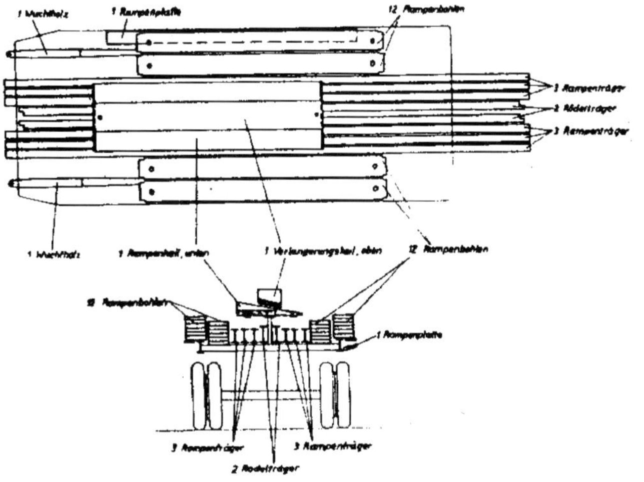

5. Beladeplan für einen Rampenwagen ([illegible])
(Rampenstrecke alter Art).

(Bild 6).

Stückzahl	Benennung	Bemerkung über die Verladung
	1. Auf dem Wagen	
24	Rampenbohlen	in 4 Belagstapeln
1	Rampenkeil	auf Aufsatzbock
6	Rampenträger	
2	Rödelträger	
1	Verlängerungskeil . . .	über den Rampenkeil verladen
2	Wuchthölzer	Gabel wird über dem vorderen Querträger des Fahrzeuges mit dem Bolzen des Wuchtholzes festgelegt
	2. Am Wagen	
1	Rampenplatte	rechte Fahrzeugseite unter dem Trittbrett
	3. Im linken Gerätekasten	
6	Bindeleinen	
4	Geländerpfosten	
2	Halteleinen	
6	Handeisen	
6	Rampenzangen	
2	Zugseile für das Ausschieben der Rampenstrecke	

Außerdem Fahrzeugzubehör gem. K. A. N. (H) Nr. 0732 am Fahrzeug und im rechten Gerätekasten.

Gesamtgewicht des Rampenwagens (Rp. Str. a./A.) . . . . 4840 kg

Leergewicht des Rampenwagens . . . . 1900 kg

Teile eines Halbpontons.

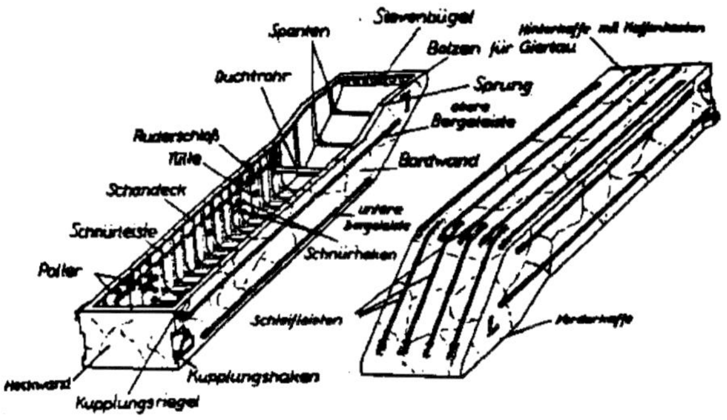

4 t-Übersetzfähre Brückengerät B mit Geländer.

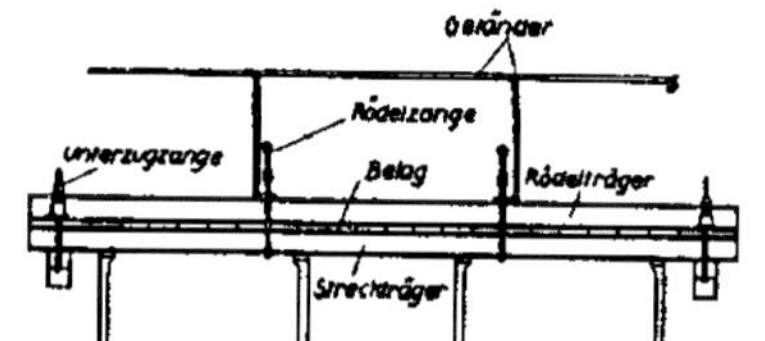

4 t-Übersetzfähre Brückengerät B.

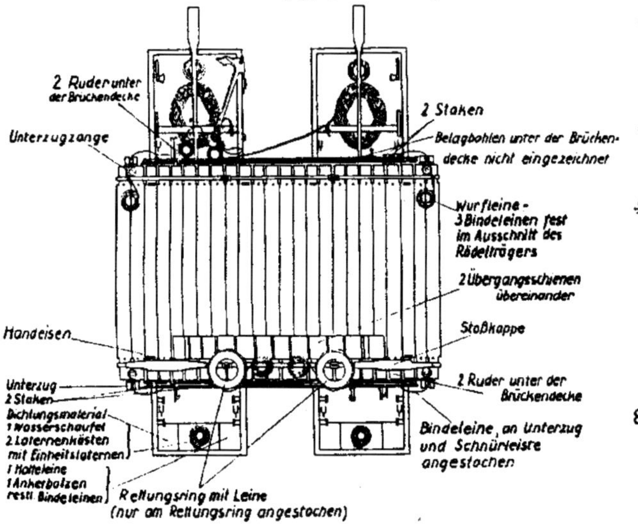

Fahrtrupps für Fähren des Brückengeräts B:

Je	Ruderer	Hilfsmannschaften	Steuerleute	Bemerkungen
4 t-Fähre (Bild 59)	4	1	2	Mindeststärke.
4 t-Fähre mit Zusatzgerät (Bild 59 a)	8	—	2	Bei starkem Strom können die Ruder mit je 2 Mann besetzt werden.
8 t-Doppelfähre (Bild 60)	6	2	2	—
8 t-Einfachfähre (Bild 61)	8	—	4	Mindeststärke.
8 t-Einfachfähre mit Zusatzgerät (Bild 61 a)	8	—	4	Bei sehr starkem Strom kann die Rudermannschaft auf 16 Mann verstärkt werden.
16 t-Fähre (Bild 62)	16	—	4	Mindeststärke bei schwachem Strom. Im allgemeinen mit Aubo fahren.

Staken einer 4 t-Fähre.

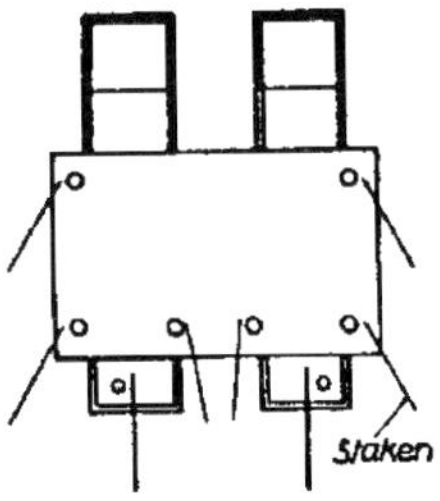

4 t-Fähre.
1 Aubo.

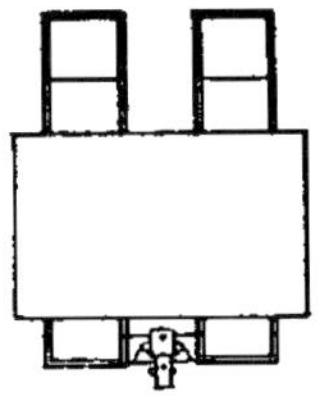

8 t-Doppelfähre.
2 Aubos.

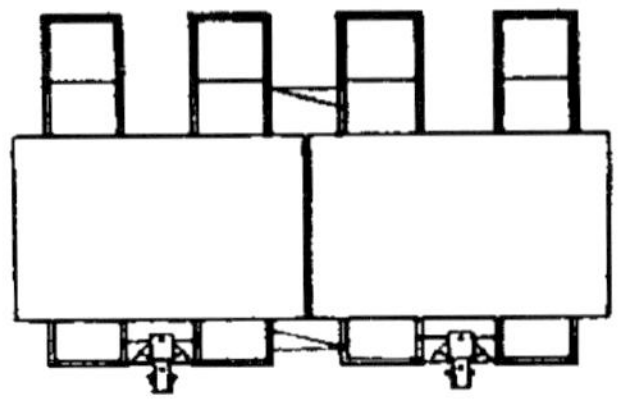

16 t-Fähre.

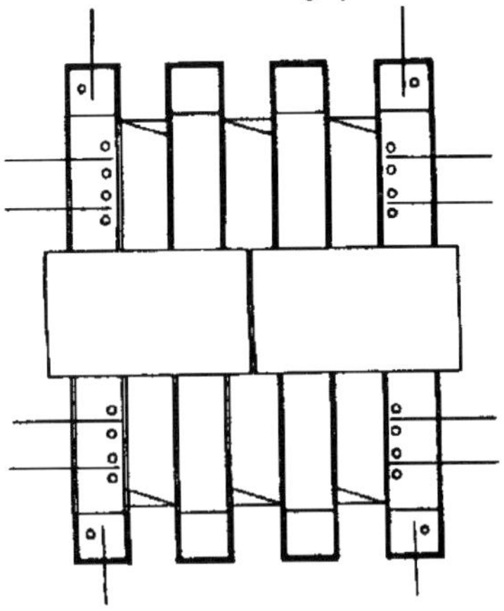

8 t-Einfachfähre.

1 Aubo.

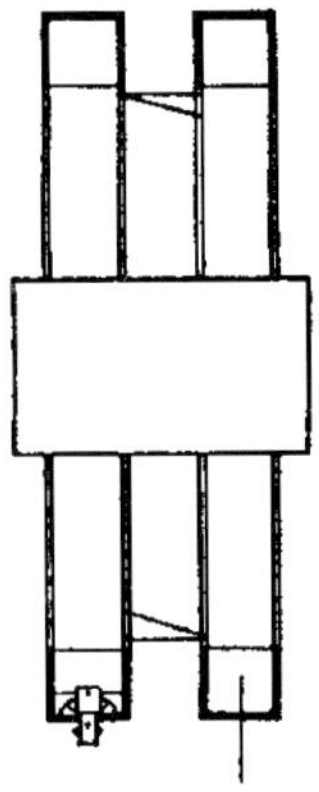

2 Aubos.

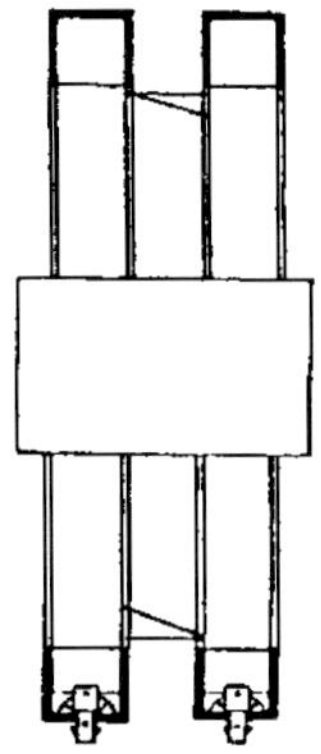

16 t-Fähre.
2 Aubos (Regel-Einbau, beste Steuerfähigkeit).

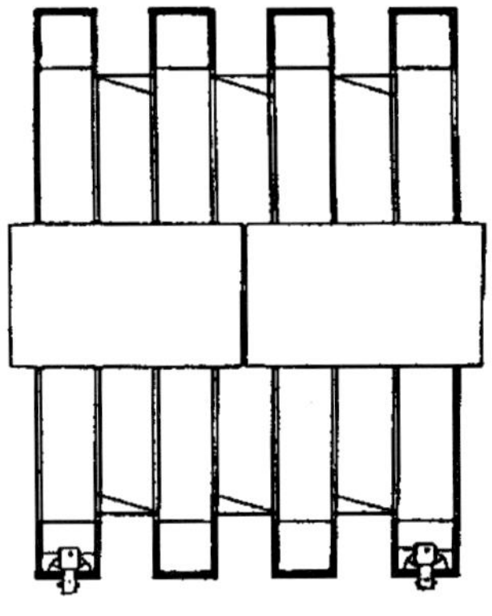

Landbrücke: Bockstrecke mit Stoßklappen und Übergangsklappe, davor 8 t-Einfachfähre angelegt.

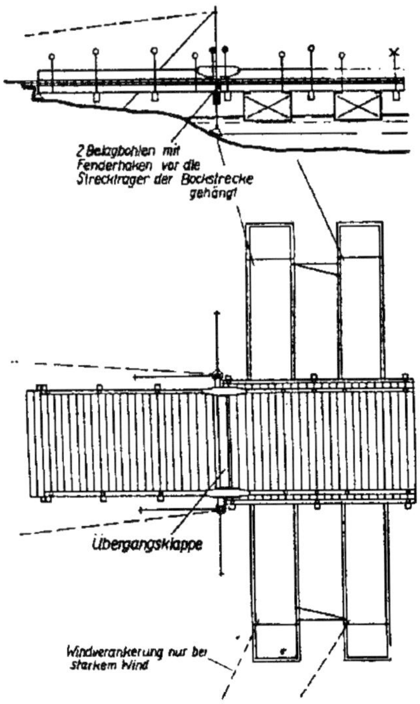

Landbrücke: Bockstrecke mit Übergangsschienen, davor 4 t-Fähre angelegt.
(Verbindung zwischen Fähre und Landbrücke durch doppelte Halteleinen (99) ist nicht eingezeichnet.)

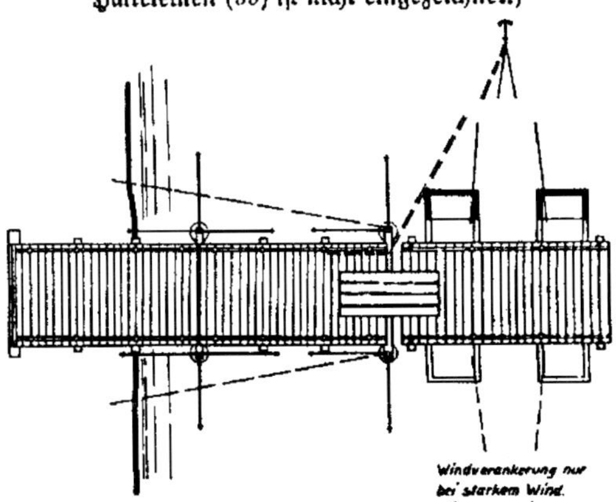

A half-pontoon of B equipment is unloaded from a pontoon wagon (Pf. 11) and carried to a river, to become part of a ferry for a military bridge. Such a load weighed 750 kilograms. So everybody had to contribute his strength. (PS)

A half-pontoon floats in the water. Here one gets a good view of the interior of the B Pontoon. (PzP)

Engineer Battalion 19 of Holzminden is rowing a whole pontoon on the Weser on the "Day of the Wehrmacht". (RK)

Engineer Battalion 236 is assembling a ferry on the Vistula in March 1941. The pontoons are being linked together. (RF)

A four-ton ferry is almost completely assembled. The rack carriers are being attached. Crossing rails are used as a connection between the riverbank and the ferry. (RF)

The four-ton ferry is finished and can be put into service. (RF)

Right: A four-ton ferry of Engineer Training Battalion 1 on the Elbe near Dessau-Rosslau in 1939. (RK)

Here four-ton ferries with additional accessories are being built. The pontoons are covered with three-color camouflage paint. Ferries with additional accessories were used for pontoon bridges when the river to be crossed had a high rate of flow. Through the greater distance from pontoon to pontoon, the bridge's resistance was decreased. (RF)

An eight-ton double ferry is loaded and casts off.

Left: Army wagons (Hf. 1/11) of an infantry rifle company are loaded onto an eight-ton double ferry.

Ferrying practice with an eight-ton double ferry on the Loire near St. Aubin. (PzP)

On a sixteen-ton ferry, a Panzer III is taken across the Don near Potemkinskaya on July 26, 1942. The ferry is just about to land at its pier. (RF)

Right: Unloading after the crossing. In front is a horsedrawn 5-cm antitank gun of the infantry. (PS)

A 10 cm Kanone 18 with an eight-ton towing tractor on a sixteen-ton ferry, being pushed to the eastern shore of the Dniepr by assault boats (9/3/41). (PS)

A sixteen-ton ferry after leaving its pier, being brought into towing position by oars, will be carried over the river—hanging on its cable—by the current. In front is the firmly anchored ferry cable, running over a drum. (Russian campaign) (PS)

A Pontoon of Type B equipment with a Ford V-8 motor that drives it by a screw propeller. (RF)

A motorboat is unloaded from Sd. Ah. 13. It had a 100-HP 6-cylinder Maybach engine. Motorboats were used to pull and push ferries across rivers as well as in bridgebuilding. (RF)

Left: The trestle for the land bridge is being placed. The trestle legs can be seen to the left and right, and the engineers are setting up the trestle spar. (RF)

The land bridge is finished. Two trestles were needed. The design can be seen clearly. From the land to the trestle are the stretch carriers, on them the roadbed planks, with the rack carriers attached with clamps that are set into the underpinnings. The railing posts are linked by ropes. The trestle legs were braced with three trestle braces. Built by Engineer Training Battalion 1 on the Elbe near Dessau-Rosslau in 1939. (RK)

Left: Now Engineer Training Battalion 1 is moving a bridge section for an eight-ton pontoon bridge, consisting of twelve half-pontoons, into the bridge position with motorboats. (RK)

Right: The bridge is finished and the "maneuver critique" is going on. (RK)

Practice for Engineer Training Battalion 1 on the Danube in the summer of 1939. An eight-ton pontoon bridge is being built. The eight stretch carriers lie on the half-pontoons, with the power pieces under them. A simple covering of boards forms the roadbed. For a 16-ton bridge, whole pontoons, 12 carriers and doubled roadway material were needed. (RK)

Right: The final work on the bridge before it is opened for traffic. A truck is already waiting on tho choro. (RK)

The bridge is finished and the personnel carriers drive to the other side. (RK)

Right: This eight-ton bridge of B material was built of accessory material from pillar 3 to the left, thus the greater distance between the pontoons. (RF)

Supplies for the French campaign roll over a pontoon bridge across the Seine. Crossing rails are laid on the pontoons.

Boats of Light Assault Boat Command 901 have reached a B bridge over the Dniepr near Shikalovka onSeptember 2, 1941. (RK)

Left: An eight-ton bridge over the Dniepr. At the right is a push flap with which the ferries were linked to form a bridge. (RF)

Engineer Battalion 80 built a pontoon bridge with a ramp section over the Weser near Holzminden. At right is the trestle section with two trestles. The floating part of the bridge is lower, so that a ramp section (slanted) was built in between. (PzP)

Above: Crossing the Dniepr on an eight-ton pontoon bridge near Bereslav. A trestle section of three trestles has been built from the shore. The pontoon bridge is lower and was linked to the trestle section by a ramp. The ramp parts were carried on a ramp wagon by the completion platoon of the bridge column. (PzP)

Left: This 16-ton bridge, 375 meters long, was built in 22 hours on June 22-23, 1940, using equipment from 14 B bridge columns of six engineer companies (1st, 2nd & 3rd Eng. Batt. 45, 2nd & 3rd Eng. Batt. 31, 3rd Eng. Batt. 2), to cross the Loire near Ancenis. (PS)

Left: A barrel wagon of Heavy Field Howitzer 18 crossing the Marne on a 16-ton pontoon bridge. (PzP)

The 2nd Company of Engineer Training Battalion 1 building a bridge over the Lys on May 26, 1940. (RK)

Left: A 16-ton B-material bridge upstream of the destroyed railroad bridge over the Dniepr at Krementshug in 1941. (RK)

A motorized column crosses a 16-ton pontoon bridge over the Dniepr, heading westward. (RK)

Engineer Regiment 413 built this "Tide Bridge" over the Scheldt near Antwerp. The difference of 6 to 8 meters between high and low tide required corrections to the makeshift land bridge every half hour. The rear ends of the half-pontoons were fitted with makeshift flow deflectors, since otherwise the swift current (4-5 meters per second at high tide) would have pushed the bridge upstream. (PS)

Right: A bridge of B material across the Dniepr. Because of shallow water at the east shore, the land bridge rests on 32 trestles. (PS)

Pontoon bridges were replaced by makeshift bridges that were built near the pontoon bridges. When they were finished, the pontoon bridges were dismantled and the materials loaded for future use. Here a B-material pontoon is loaded onto the pontoon trailer (Pf. 11) by the Engineer Training Battalion in 1939. (RF)

Bridge Material C
(from service manual D 516)

Bridge Material C allowed the building of bridges and ferries for loads up to four tons. With it, the following could be built:

- Landing stages on small float sacks,
- Landing stages on half-pontoons up to 70 meters,
- Bridges on whole pontoons up to 140 meters,
- Two-ton ferries,
- Four-ton ferries,
- Single special ferries,
- Double special ferries,
- Four-ton bridges,
- Special bridges of 84 meters, 42 meters of them floating.

The half-pontoons were made of wood or light sheet metal, were 3.9 m long, 1.67 m wide above, had sidewalls 0.72 m high, their greatest height was 0.82 m, and when made of wood they weighed 232 kilograms. They could be stacked on each other.

The bridge structure consisted of two long carriers made of steel, with a bed 60 cm wide and 7 meters long.

The bridge was able to carry:

- Infantry of up to three marching columns,
- Light artillery, horsedrawn, drivers dismounted,
- Single vehicles up to four tons, with axle pressure up to 2.6 tons.

For ferry building, two whole pontoons were placed side by side and occupied by two men each. The material was installed in the following order: Preliminary construction with two medium bridge plates—staking toward the water—setting off—staking toward the land—installation of remaining bridge plates—installation of the edge carriers—installation of the undersections.

Loading and unloading the ferries took place over land bridges or crossing rails.

In Bridge Column C, two crossing rails for 5.3-ton loads were carried on each pontoon wagon.

The land bridge consisted of the shore timbers laid on the riverbank, the trestle stretch leading to the trestle, the trestle, and the crossing stretch to the first pontoon. For use with ferries, crossing rails were laid between the trestles and ferries.

Of the sixteen large float bags carried, float-bag ferries of two- or four-ton capacity could also be constructed with the materials.

A footbridge made of Small Float Bag 34s and bridge planks of the C material lets the infantry cross a river. (RF)

 (734) **Br. Kol. C (mot).**

Gruppe Führer: 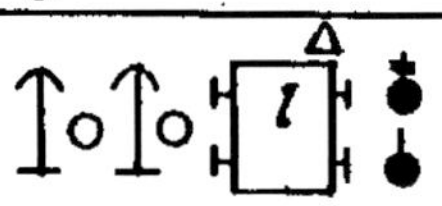

1. u. 2. (Pont.) Zug je:

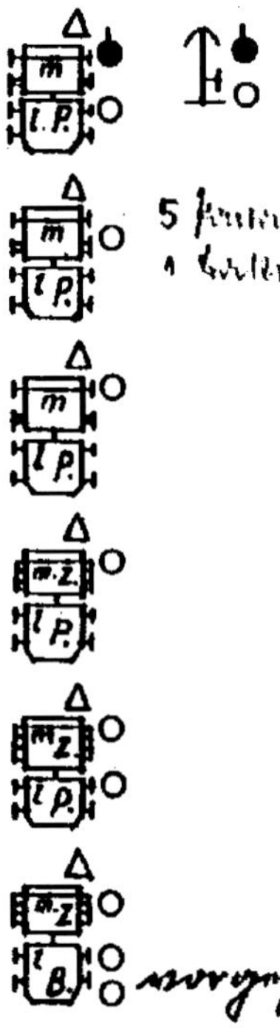

5 Pontonwagen
1 Bockwagen

ferner vorgesehen
1 Wagen m. 3 Sturmbooten

Ergänzungszug:

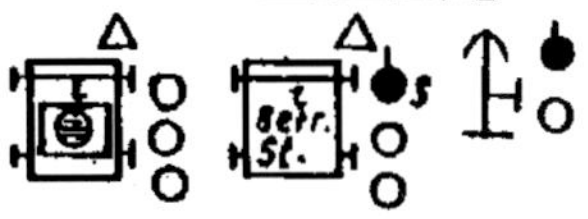

V.-u. G.-Troß:

Gesamtstärke:

1 Offizier,	1 l. Pkw.,
7 Unteroffiziere,	6 m. Zg. Kw.,
45 Pioniere (dav. 20 Kflf.),	6 m. gl. Lkw.,
	3 l. Lkw.
	5 Krad (dav. 3 m. Beiw.)
	12 Anhänger (10 Ponton, 2 Bock.)

Marschlänge i. Halten:

Ganze Kolonne ohne V.-u. G. Tr.	rd.	260 m
Pontonzug	"	110 "
Erg. Zug	"	25 "
V.-u. G.-Troß	"	10 "

Nachr. Gerät u. Leist.-Fähigkeit:

1 Sprechstelle, 1000 m l. Feldkabel,
2 Satz Flußkabel (insg. 2000 m)

Gerät der Br. Kol. C (mot)

~~(neu)~~

Übersetzmittel:

Kl. Floßsäcke	~~56~~ 48
Gr. "	~~8~~ 16

Sperrmittel:

K.-Rolle	12

Personal nicht zum Bedienen, sondern zur Pflege u. Verwaltung des Geräts. Im Frieden nur Geräte-Einheit, kein Personal.

Steg auf kleinen Floßsäcken

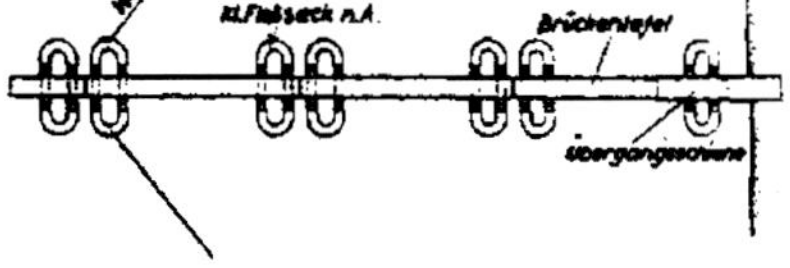

Steg auf Halbpontons

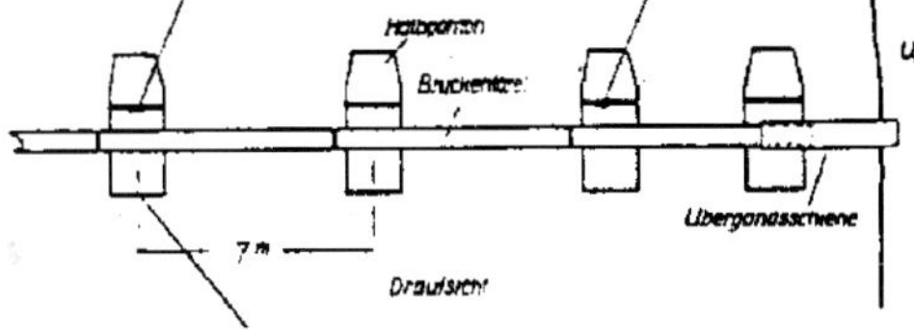

Above: Light Trestle Wagon (Pf. 14) (D 600).

Below: Light Pontoon Wagon (Pf. 15) (D 600).

Beladung des Bockwagens.

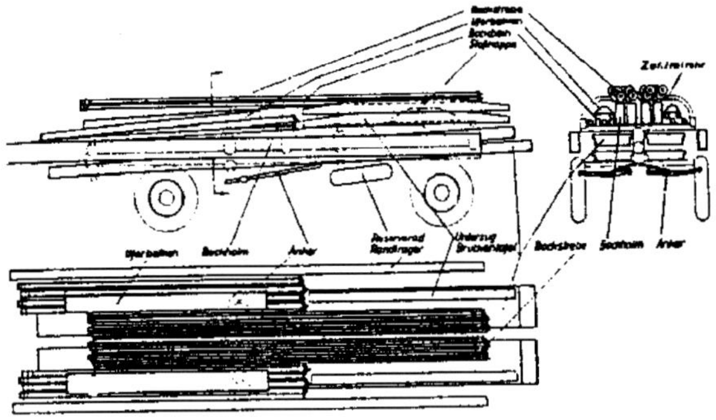

Beladung des Bockwagens.

Brückentafel	4	Bindeleine	20
Randträger	2	Einfahrzeichen	1
Stoßkappe	2	Klauenbeil	2
Unterzug	4	lange Kreuzhacke ..	1
Bockholm	4	Laternenkasten	2
Bockbein	8	Maßstab 2 m lang	2
Bockstrebe	16	Richtleine	1
Bockwinde	4	Schlegel	2
Fußscheibe	8	langer Spaten	1
Geländerholz	4	Wasserwaage	1
Handeisen	8	Aussteckflagge	8
Uferbalkenpfahl ...	20	Uferbalken	2
Ankerleine	2		

Gewicht unbeladen etwa 1400 kg,
» beladen etwa 4300 kg.

Stechruder für Brückengerät C.

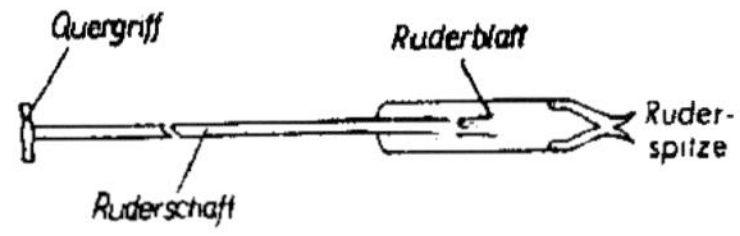

Beladung des Pontonwagens.

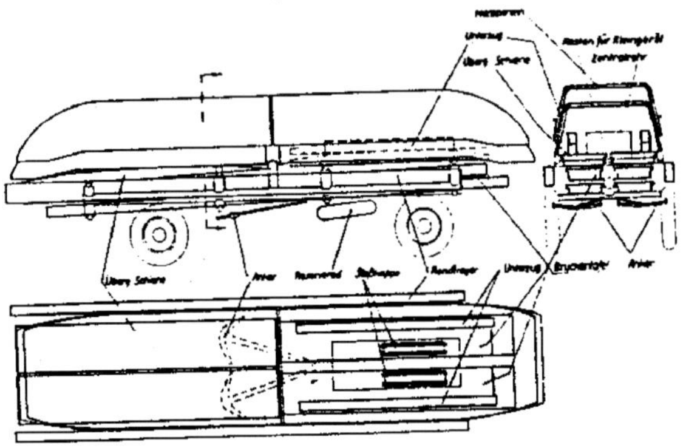

Beladung des Pontonwagens.

Halbponton	4	Bindeleine	20
Scherhaken	2	Beutel mit Dichtungsmaterial ..	2
Brückentafel	4	Klauenbeil	2
Randträger	2	lange Kreuzhacke...	1
Stoßkappe	2	Laternenkasten	2
Unterzug	4	Stechruder	12
Geländerholz	4	langer Spaten.....	1
Handeisen	8	Wasserschaufel	4
Anker	2	Übergangsschiene ..	2
Ankerbolzen	1	Halteleine 30 m ...	4
Ankerrödel	4	Rettungsring mit Leine	2
Ankerleine	4		

Gewicht unbeladen etwa 1400 kg,
» beladen etwa 4300 kg.

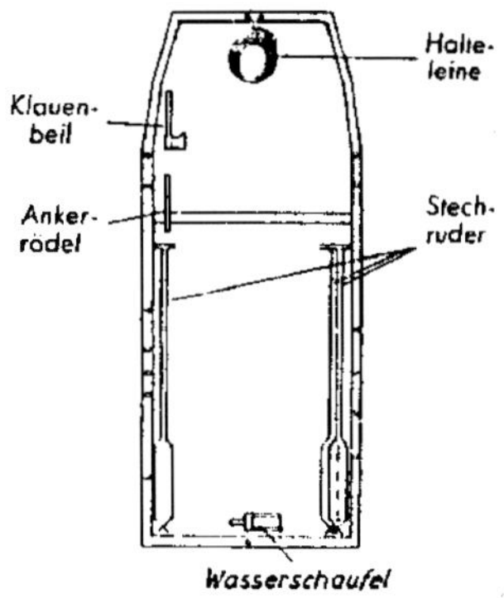

Ausrüstung des Halbpontons:
3 Stechruder,
1 Halteleine,
1 Duchtholz,
1 Ankerrödel,
1 Wasserschaufel,
außerdem für je 2 Halbpontons 1 Klauenbeil und 1 Rettungsring mit Leine.

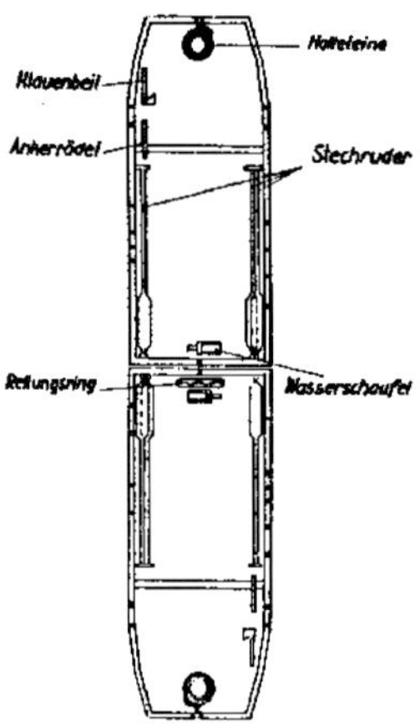

Ausrüstung des Ganzpontons:
6 Stechruder,
2 Klauenbeile,
2 Halteleinen,
2 Duchthölzer,
2 Ankerrödel,
2 Wasserschaufeln,
1 Rettungsring mit Leine.

Laufbrücke, Regelbau.

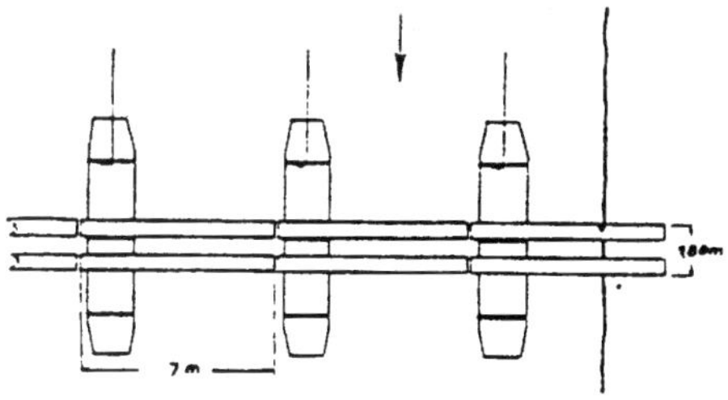

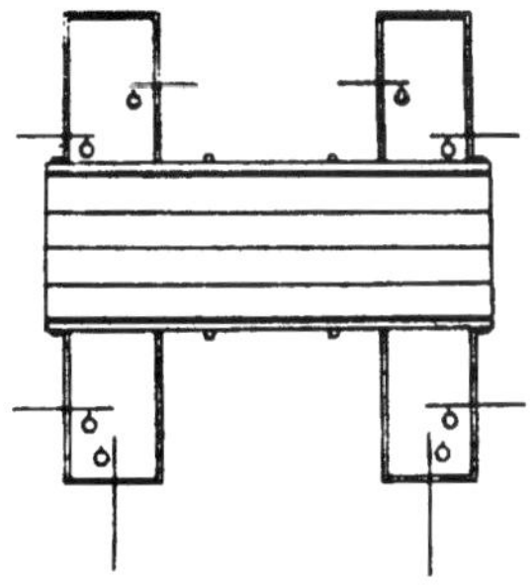

Bild 71.
2 t-Fähre.

Bild 72. **4 t-Fähre.**

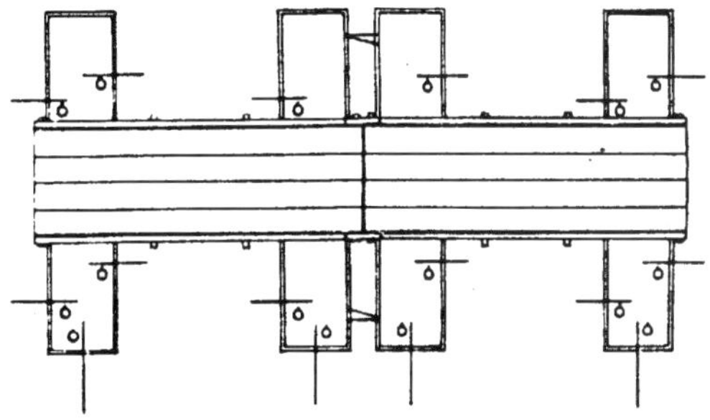

2 t-Fähre, fertig zum Einfahren.

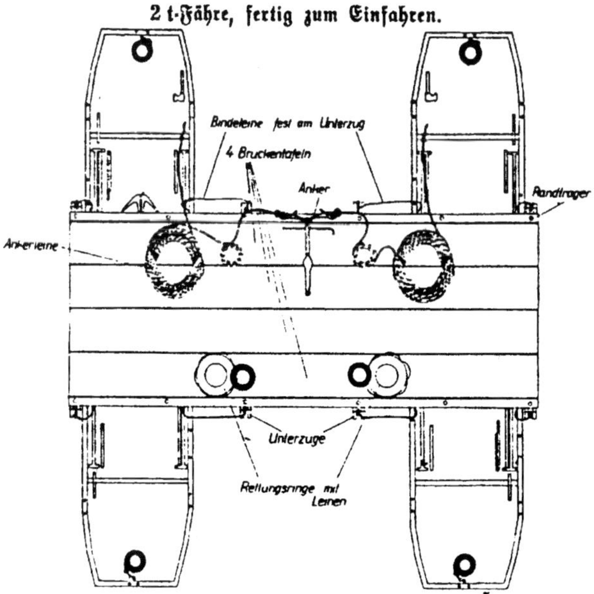

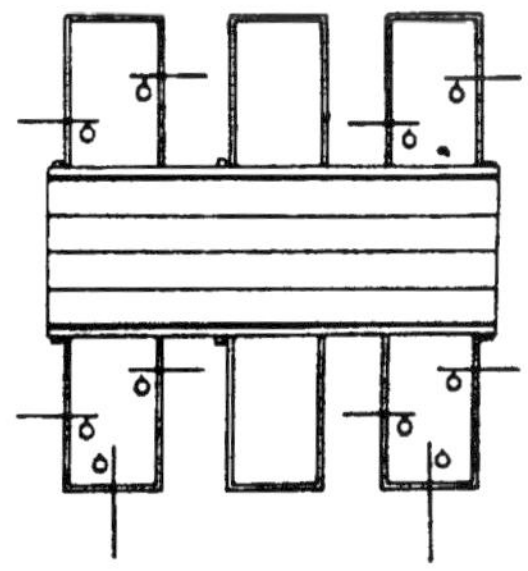

Bild 73.
Einfache Sonderfähre.

Doppelte Sonderfähre.

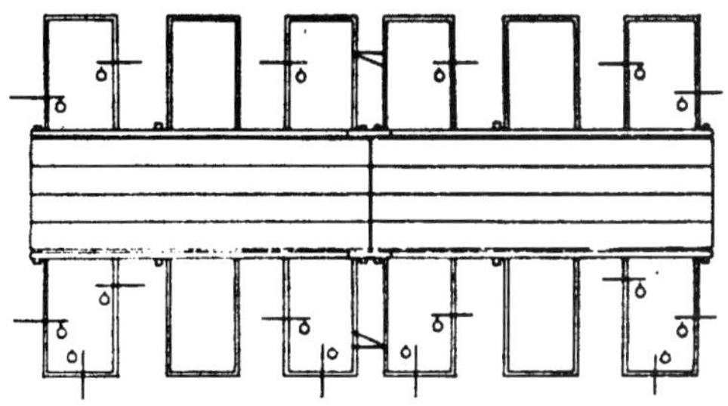

4 t-Brücke, Draufsicht.

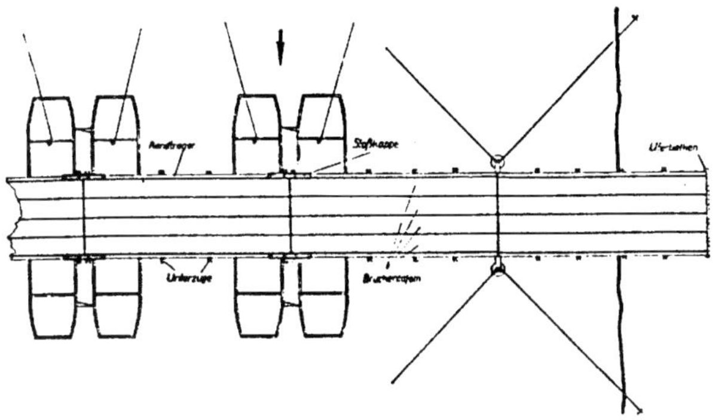

4 t-Brücke. Streckenweiser Bau mit Truppangabe.

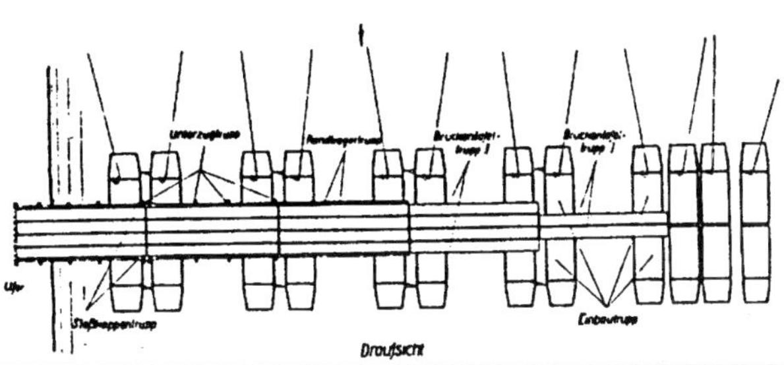

A Bridge Column C during a marching pause. (RK)

Left: Magirus Type M 30 trucks were used for towing. (RK)

Bridgebuilding begins. The half-pontoons were unloaded from the pontoon wagon (Pf. 15). (RF)

The bridge plate, seven meters long, is laid on the whole pontoon of C material by Engineer Battalion 35. (PzP)

Left: A footbridge on half-pontoons is built. (RF)

A single special ferry of SS Engineer Battalion 7 "Prince Eugene" on the Drina, in Yugoslavia in 1944. (RK)

A bridge over the Aisne-Oise Canal, built of C material by the 3./Engineer Battalion 72 in June 1940. (PzP)

Right: Bridgebuilding practice by Engineer Battalion 35 near Suvalki Zipfel in preparation for the Russian campaign. (PzP)

A pontoon bridge of C material across the Bug in the sector hf the 252nd Infantry Division. (PzP)

Bridge Material K n.A.
(from H.Dv. 220/3c)

The K. n. A. bridge material was a readymade box-carrier device for heavy loads up to 16 tons, including tracked vehicles up to 20 tons.

The box-carrier material consisted of lattice beams. The end piece was 5.02 meters long, 48 cm wide, one meter high at one end and 27 cm at the other. It weighed 418 kg. The central piece was five meters long, one meter high and 48 cm wide. It weighed 498 kg.

It was used mainly for fast bridging of narrow waterways, deep ditches, holes in off-road terrain and destroyed bridge openings, to ferry heavy individual vehicles, and to overcome rough shore conditions when linked with Bridge Material B.

With the materials of a half-platoon, the following could be built:
- one 16-ton bridge of 19.20-meter support width, or
- one 16-ton bridge of 14.40-meter support width, or
- one 16-ton bridge of 9.60-meter support width.

With the materials of a platoon, the following could be built:
- one 16-ton bridge on floating intermediate supports with
- 38.40-meter bridge length, or
- 33.60-meter bridge length, or
- 28.80-meter bridge length, or
- 24.00-meter bridge length.

With the materials of a whole column, the following couild be built:
- one 16-ton bridge on floating intermediate supports, including a double block of
- 78.80-meter bridge length.

The K material could also be used as a land bridge with a bridge of B material. The usable bridge width was 3.50 meters.

PONTOONS

The end pontoon was made of aluminum, some 5.5 meters long, 2.2 meters wide, and had one meter of height in its horizontal part. The bow part had a rise of 10 cm and was drawn in. It weighed 380 kilograms.

The middle pontoon was made of aluminum, some 4 meters long, 2.2 meters wide and one meter high. It had vertical bow walls with couplings, and weighed 480 kg.

Two end pontoons and one middle pontoon were coupled together to form one pontoon. These three pieces were carried on a pontoon wagon.

FERRY BUILDING

The box-carrier device was only used for crossing ferrying in exceptional cases. Crossing ferries were always built as short ferries if there was no possibility of using them later in bridges, in which case the long construction was called for. There were short, medium and long sixteen-ton ferries.

A short 16-ton ferry is assembled. Three pontoons, consisting of two ends and one middle piece, are in place. The carrier end-pieces rest on the middle section of each pontoon. (RF)

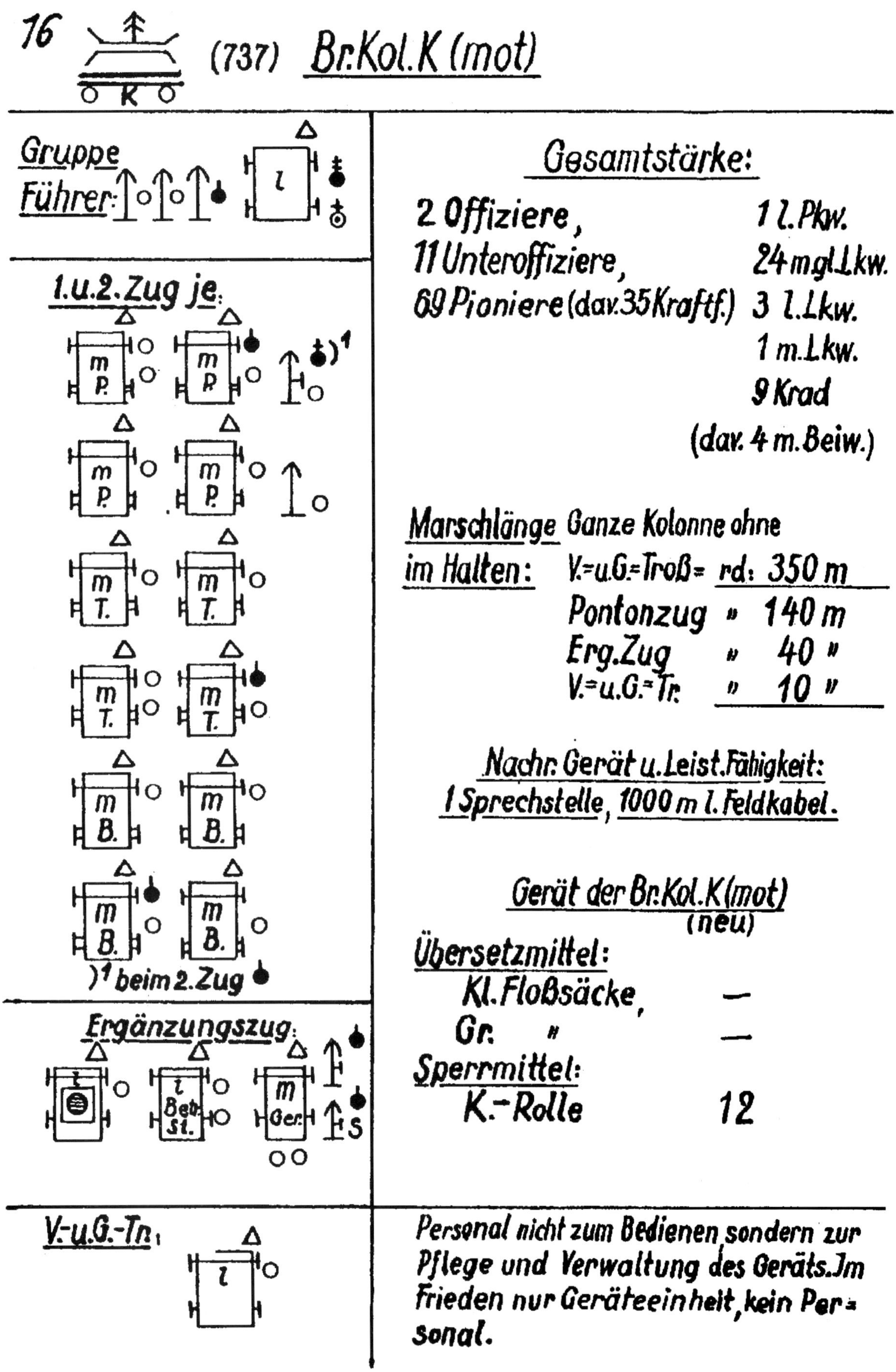

Diese Gliederung aus dem Jahr 1937 ist hier noch ohne den Bockwagen 39, der Bestandteil jedes Halbzuges wurde, angegeben. Außerdem fehlen 1 m. Lkw. als Gerätewagen, 2 Motorboot-Anhänger und 3m. Lkw. für Floßsäcke. Mit dieser Ausstattung lautete die Bezeichnung Brückenkolonne K (mot) n. A.

A K material pontoon wagon, Mercedes L 4500 A, of the "H.G." Paratroop Armored Division. (PzP)

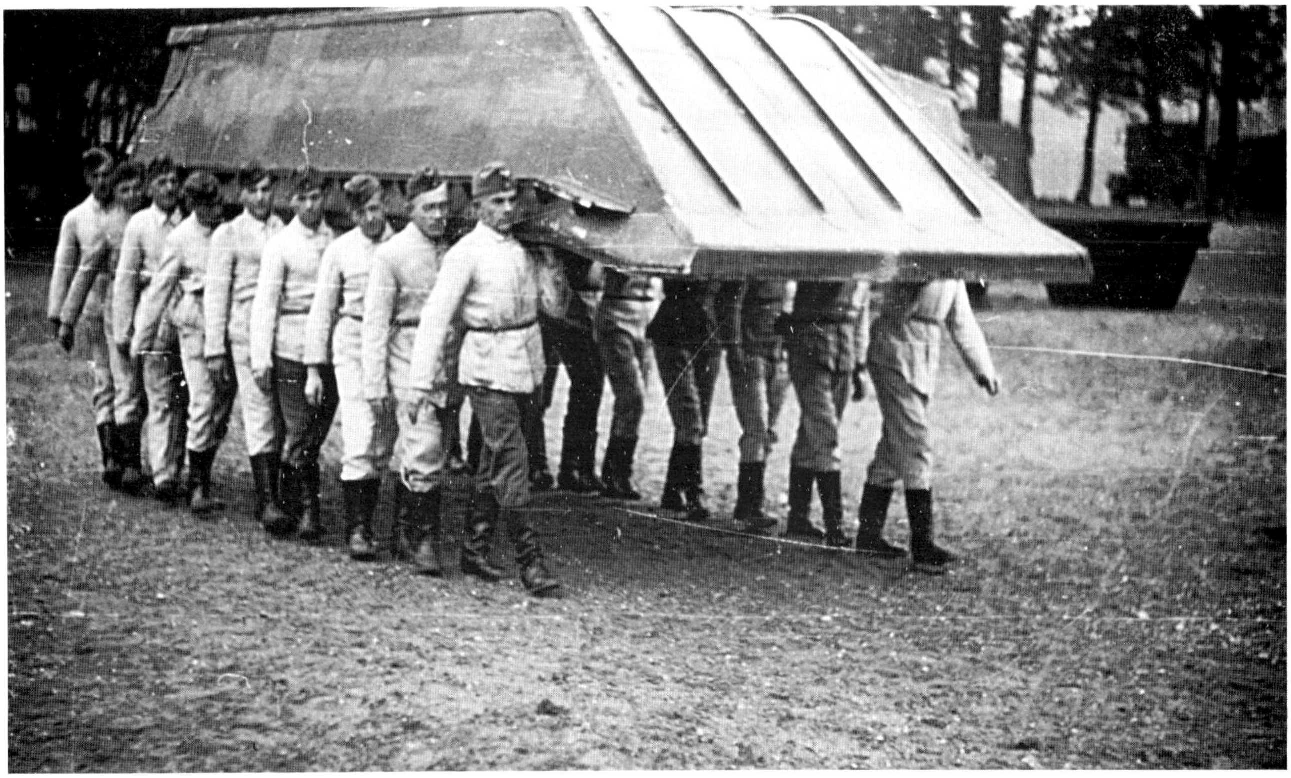

Ferry building by Armored Engineer Battalion 49. An end piece of Bridge Material K is carried to the water by eighteen engineers. (RF)

Pontonwagen.

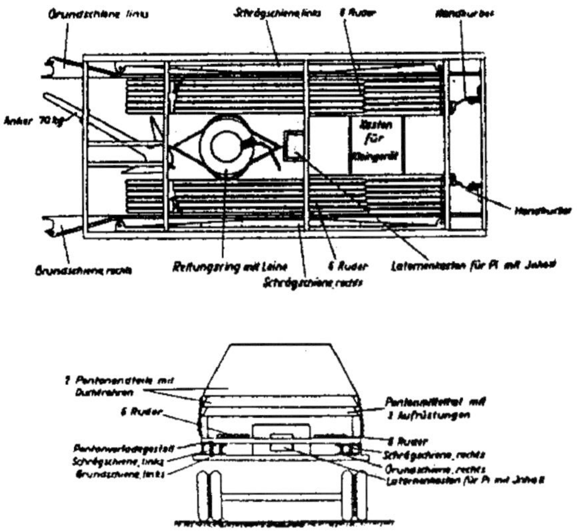

Trägerwagen.

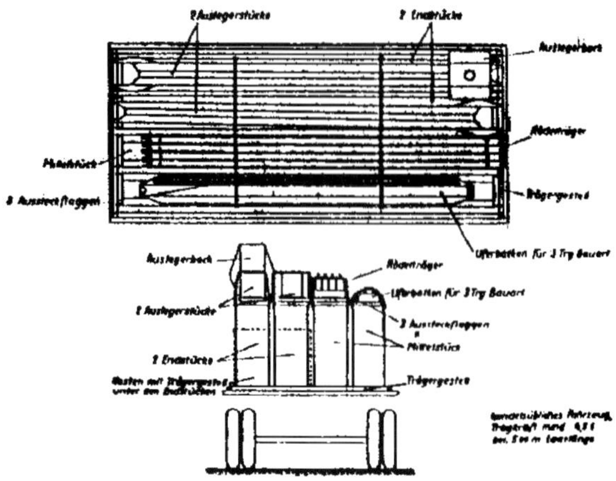

BELADUNG:
1 Anker 70 kg
2 Pontonendteile
1 Pontonmittelteil
1 Pontonverladegestell
1 Rettungsring mit Leine
12 Ruder

BELADUNG:
2 Auslegerböcke
1 Auslegerrolle
2 Auslegerstücke
2 Endstücke
2 Mittelstücke
2 Rollenböcke
1 Trägergestell
1 Uferbalken

Ganzponton des Brückengeräts K.

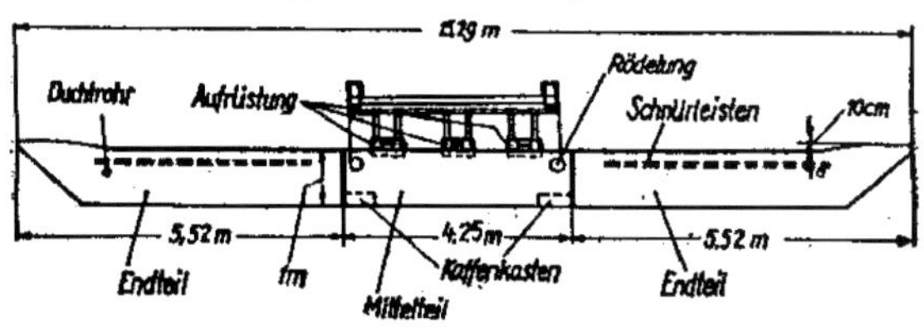

Belagwagen.

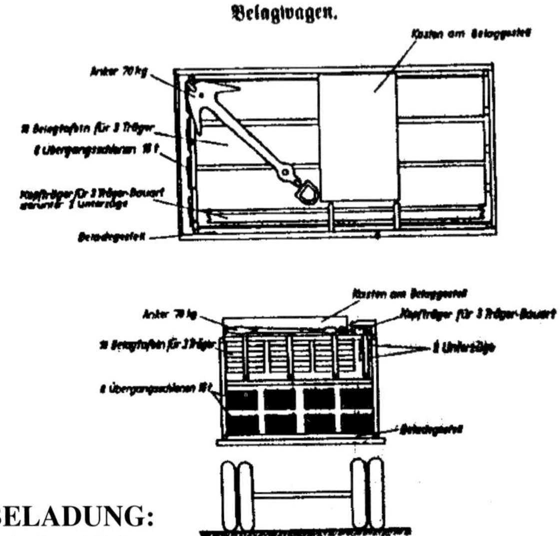

Bockwagen.

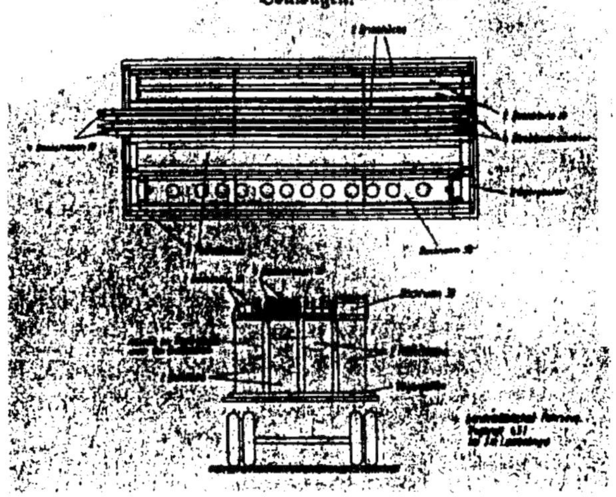

BELADUNG:
1 Anker 70 kg
18 Belagtafeln für 3 Träger
5 Geländerstützen
1 Kopfträger
8 Übergangsschienen 16 t
2 Unterzüge

BELADUNG:
2 Bockbeine 39
1 Bockholm 39
4 Bockstreben 39
2 Bockwinden
2 Endstücke
2 Fußscheiben 39
2 Mittelstücke
1 Trägergestell

Mit dem Gerät eines Halbzuges kann gebaut werden[2]):

a) Eine 16 t-Brücke von 19,20 m Stützweite mit Einbau von 2 Endstücken und 2 Mittelstücken in jeden Träger (Bild 1)

Bild 1.

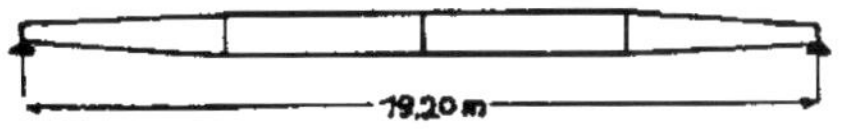

oder

b) eine 16 t-Brücke von 14,40 m Stützweite bei Einbau von 2 Endstücken und 1 Mittelstück in jeden Träger (Bild 2)

Bild 2.

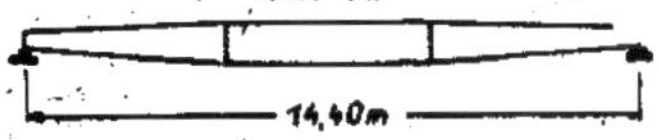

oder

c) zwei 16 t-Brücken von 9,60 m Stützweite bei Einbau von 1 End- und 1 Mittelstück in jeden Träger (Bild 3)[1])

Bild 3.

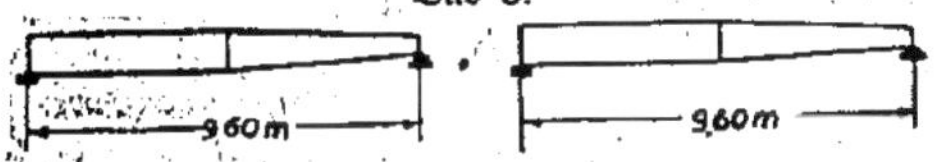

oder

d) eine 16 t-Brücke von 9,60 m Stützweite bei Einbau von 2 Endstücken in jeden Träger (Bild 4)[2])

Bild 4.

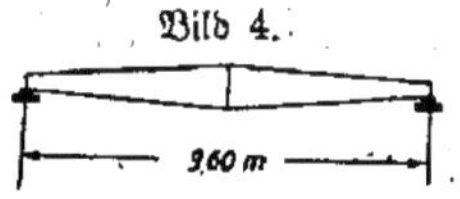

und

eine 16 t-Brücke von 9,60 m Stützweite bei Einbau von 2 Mittelstücken in jeden Träger, wobei das Festlegen der Mittelstücke gegen Verschieben auf Behelfsuferbalken besonders zu beachten ist (Bild 5)[2]).

Bild 5.

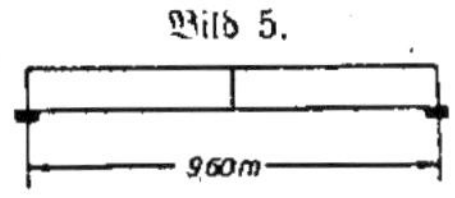

Mit dem Gerät eines Zuges kann gebaut werden[1]):

a) Eine 16 t-Brücke auf schwimmenden Zwischenstützen mit 38,40 m Brückenlänge (Bild 7)

Bild 7.

oder

b) — unter Weglassen einzelner Mittel- und Endstücke — eine 16 t-Brücke auf schwimmenden Zwischenstützen mit einer Brückenlänge von 33,60 m (Bild 8)

Bild 8.

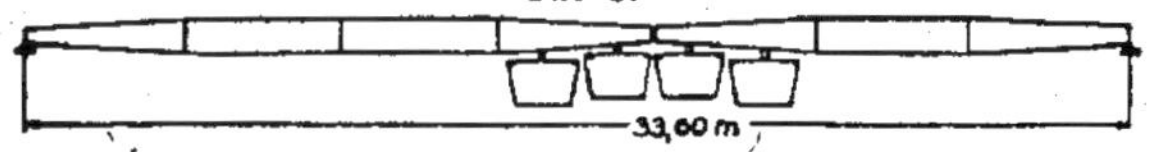

oder

eine 16 t-Brücke auf schwimmenden Zwischenstützen mit einer Brückenlänge von 28,80 m (Bild 9)

Bild 9.

oder

eine 16 t-Brücke auf schwimmenden Zwischenstützen mit einer Brückenlänge von 24,00 m (Bild 10)

Bild 10.

Wenn in der Nähe der Ufer eine Wassertiefe von mindestens 0,80 m vorhanden ist, können durch eine lange 16 t-Fähre unter Verwendung der 16 t-Übergangsschienen als Landbrücken Wasserläufe bis etwa 25 m Breite überbrückt werden (Bild 11).

Bild 11.

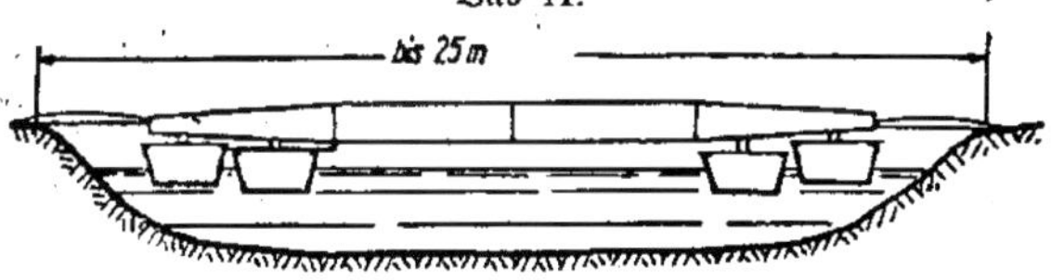

Mit dem Gerät der ganzen Kolonne können gebaut werden[1]):

Eine 16 t-Brücke auf schwimmenden Zwischenstützen unter Einbau eines Doppelbockes von 76,80 m Brückenlänge (Bild 12)

Bild 12.

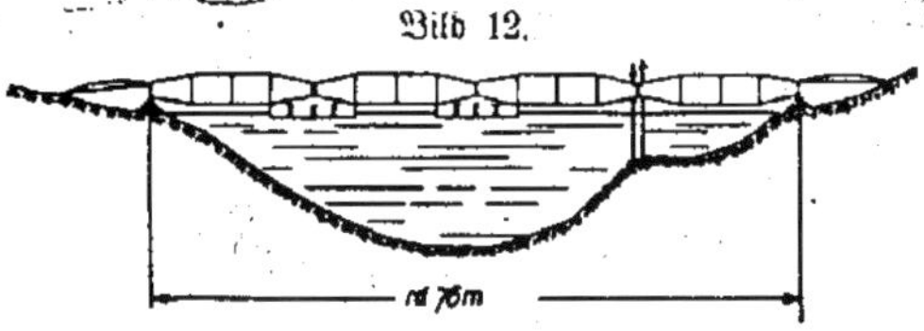

oder

b) zwei 16 t-Brücken auf schwimmenden Zwischenstützen mit 38,40 m Brückenlänge (Bild 7)

oder

c) unter Weglassen einzelner Mittel- und Endstücke zwei 16 t-Brücken mit Brückenlängen von 33,60 m (Bild 8)

oder

zwei 16 t-Brücken mit Brückenlängen von 28,80 m (Bild 9)

oder

zwei 16 t-Brücken mit Brückenlängen von 24,00 m (Bild 10)

Zusammen- und Vorbau der Träger.

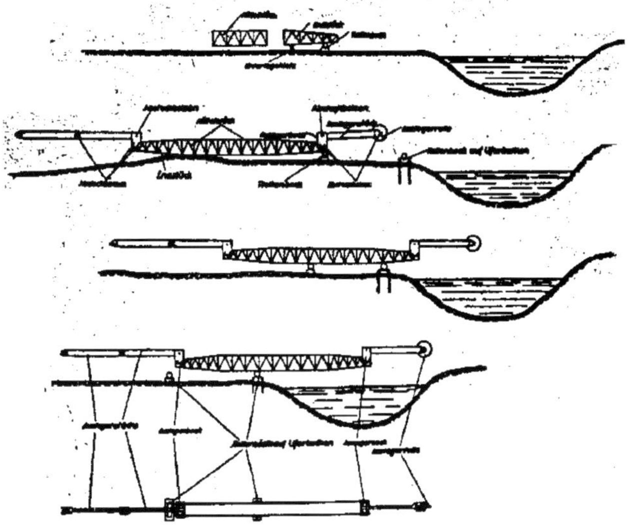

16 t-Uferbrücke mit 19,20 m Stützweite.

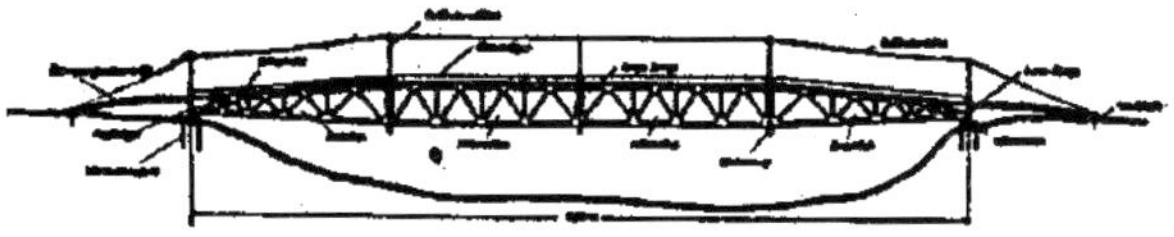

16 t-Uferbrücke mit 9,60 m Stützweite (Ausnahmebauart).

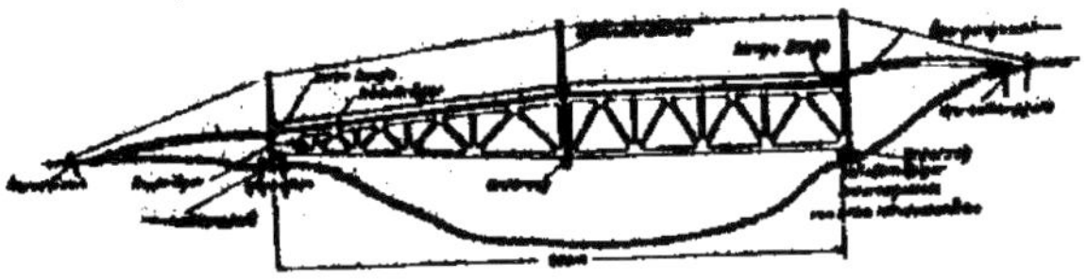

Brücke mit Doppelbock als Zwischenstütze.

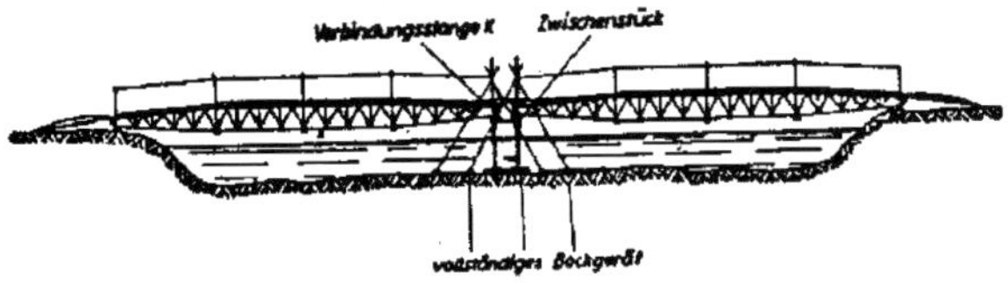

Querschnitt.

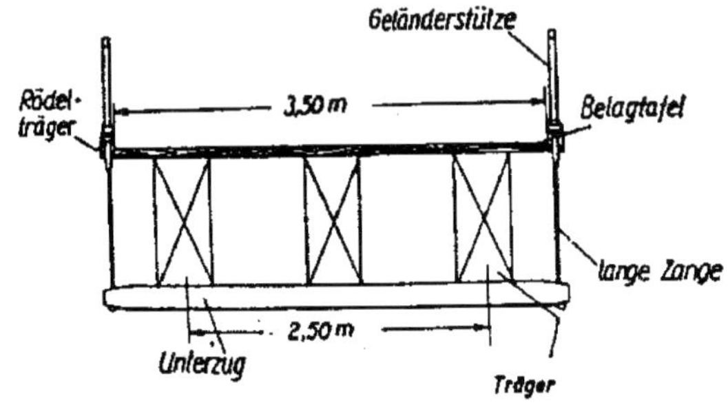

Verwendung einer K-Strecke als Landbrücke bei einer Brücke aus B-Gerät.

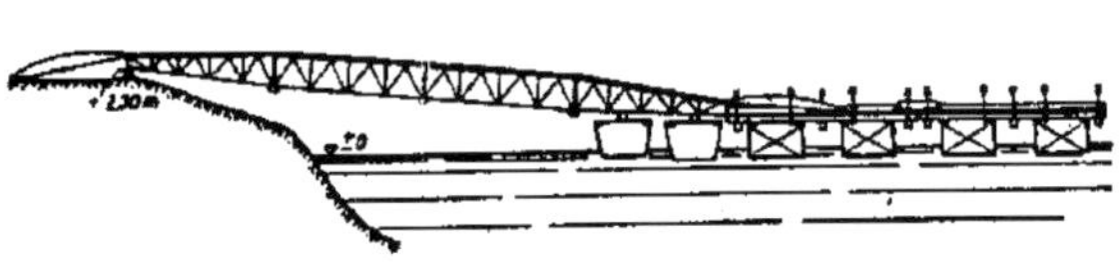

Verbindung zwischen Brückengerät B und Brückengerät K in Bockstrecken.

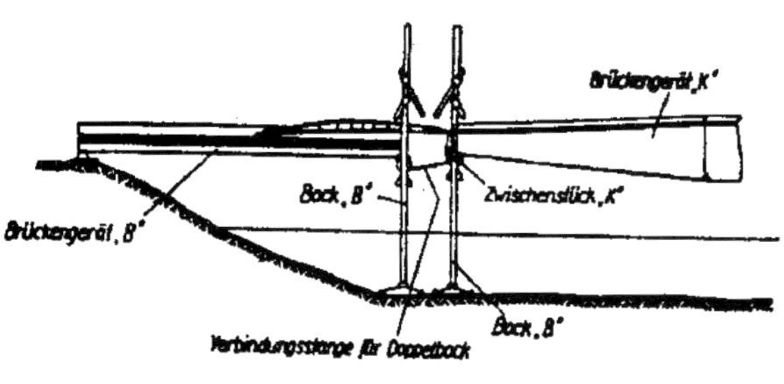

Fährenbau.

Ausrüstung einer mittleren 16 t-Fähre.

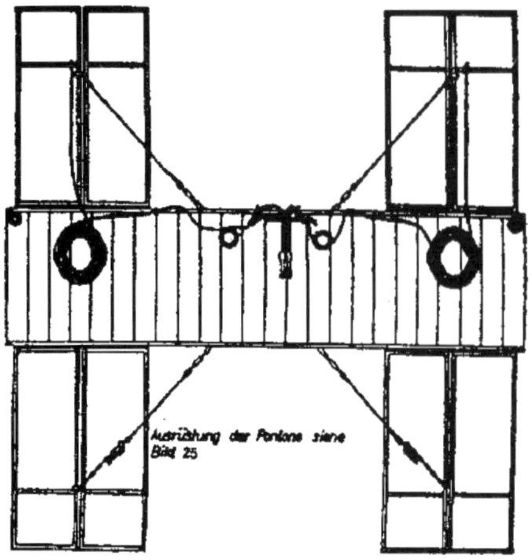

Kurze 16 t-Fähre.

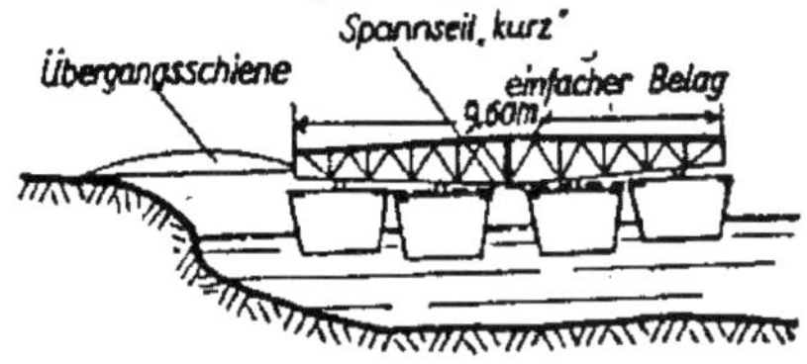

Mittlere 16 t-Fähre.

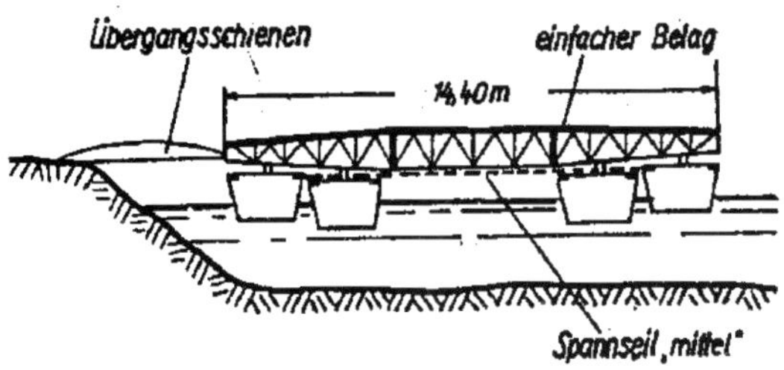

Lange 16 t-Fähre.

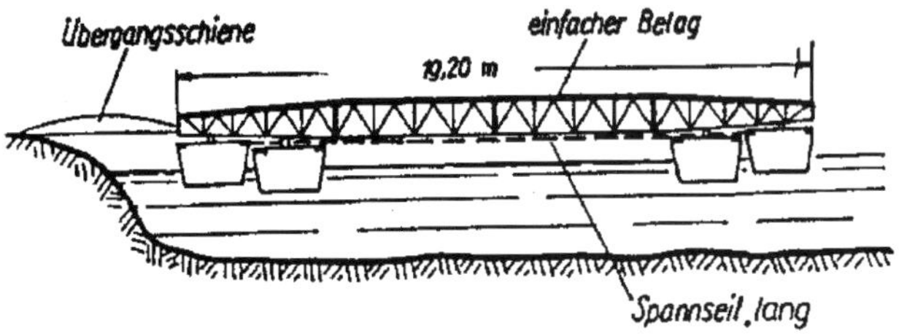

16 t-Brücke aus zwei Fähren mit Übergangsschienen als Landanschlüsse.

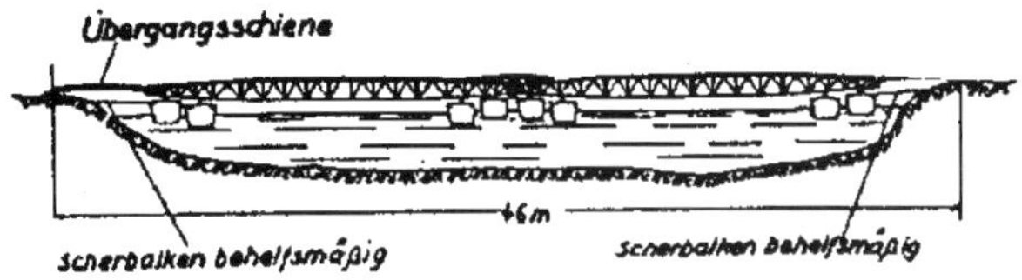

Draufsicht

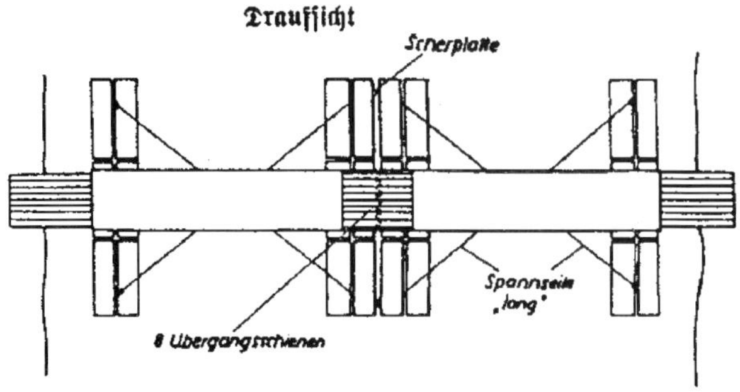

The fourth pontoon is attached and the ferry is ready for use. (RF)

Armored Engineer Battalion 1 of the SS "L.A.H." Division learning to use K material from Army engineers, August 1940. The extender trestle, extender piece and extender roll on the carrier end piece can be seen. (RK)

Bridgebuilding practice by SS Armored Engineer Battalion 1 at Metz in the late autumn of 1940. (RK)

Armored engineers of the "H.G." Division building a bridge. At right are the three lattice carriers; the roadbed pieces are being attached. (PzP)

The bridge is finished. A medium off-road-capable truck carries out the load testing.

The Ingulex Bridge near Krivoi-Rog was blown up by the Russians. The ruined part was bridged over with K material by Armored Engineer Battalion 86. (PzP)

Above: A land bridge of K material as a pier for B-material ferries. (RK)

Right: A 16-ton bridge on floating intermediate supports and trestles. The contact points of the box carriers have been bridged over with crossing rails. (PzP